The cat loves fish, but hates wet feet.
>   Medieval proverb

My sister crying, our maid howling, our
cat wringing her hands.
>   Two Gentlemen of Verona
>   act 2, scene 3, line 7

The human race may be divided into people who love cats and people who hate
them; the neutrals being few in numbers,
and, for intellectual and moral reasons,
not worth considering.
>   Ascribed to "an acute thinker"
>   by Agnes Repplier (1855 - 1950)
>   The Fireside Sphinx

A cat can climb down from a tree without
the assistance of the fire department or
any other agency. The proof is that no one
has ever seen a cat skeleton in a tree.
>   Unknown

Another Fawcett Crest Book
by Robert Byrne

THE 637 BEST THINGS ANYBODY EVER SAID

CAT SCAN

All of the best from
the literature of cats

Compiled and Edited by
Robert Byrne and Teressa Skelton

Foreword by Cyra McFadden

Illustrations by Missy Dizick

FAWCETT CREST • NEW YORK

Acknowledgments

The editors are grateful to the following for permission to reprint copyrighted material:

William Rossa Cole, for four poems, including "What Could It Be," which first appeared in *A Cat Hater's Handbook*, Pinnacle Books, 1982; Coward, McCann & Geoghegan, Inc., for the excerpt from the Foreword to *Cats in Prose and Verse*, by Nelson Antrim Crawford, 1947; Crown Publishers, Inc., for excerpts from *Honorable Cat*, by Paul Gallico; copyright © 1972 by Paul Gallico and Mathemata Anstalt; Doubleday, for excerpts from *Cat People*, copyright © 1978 by C. William Hayward, Jr.; Gerald Fitzgerald, for excerpts from his liner notes for the London Records album *Classical Cats*, 1982; Harper & Row, for excerpts from *The Cat's Pajamas: A Charming and Clever Compendium of Feline Trivia*, by Leonore Fleischer; copyright © 1982 by Leonore Fleischer; New Century Publishers, Inc., for the recipes from *The Disgusting, Despicable Cat Cookbook*, copyright © 1982 by

John Eaton and Julie Kurnitz; Macmillan Publishing Co., Inc., for "Last Words to a Dumb Friend," from *Complete Poems of Thomas Hardy*, edited by James Gibson, 1978; The New York Times, for "Tales for Cats," by Russell Baker, which appeared August 9, 1981, "Cats I Have Known and Loathed," by Gilbert Millstein, which appeared March 13, 1977, and "No More Mr. Nice Guy," by Russell Baker, which appeared August 15, 1982; Helen Powers, for excerpts from *The Biggest Little Cat Book in the World*, published by Grosset & Dunlap in 1977; Simon & Schuster, for excerpts from *Particularly Cats*, copyright © 1967 by Doris Lessing Productions, Ltd.; Derek Williamson, for "Mad Anthony," from *The Literary Cat*, by Walter Chandoha, J. B. Lippincott Co.; Workman Publishing Co., for "Sphinx and Cheops" (called "Pyramid Power" here), by Jurgen Gothe, "Seeing-Eye Cats," by Brian McConnachie, "The Cat in Music," by Claire Necker, and "Dogs Are Not Purrfect," by Robert Stearns, all of which appeared in slightly longer form in *Cat Catalog*, 1976.

For Sean, Veronica, and Pushkin

Almost everybody, it seems to me, sooner or later writes a cat book.

> R. L. Duffus
> (who yielded to temptation in 1967)

Contents

Foreword

Who needs another cat book? No one, probably, but then, except for the chronically mice-ridden, no one needs cats. For all-round utility, they're about as useful as water-soluble sponges.

Cats won't bring in the morning paper or clean up the leftovers from your dinner, unless the main course was canned cat food, and have no talents aside from killing the first robin of spring and leaving the corpse on your porch. When they're affectionate, which is rarely, they jump up on your chest and inflict puncture wounds. Give a cat a scratching post and he'll shred your oriental rug instead, oblivious to claws and effect. Because the whole animal is propelled by a brain the size of a walnut, cats aren't known for their higher intelligence. The resident cat in my house, who holds the West Coast record for shedding, can spend an hour staring at the wall. He's old, and that may have something to do with it, but in his prime he was never a wit nor an original thinker.

As Robert Byrne points out in his introduction to this entertaining book, cat mania is nonetheless a widespread disease, more fashionable, even, than hypoglycemia. I can't explain the epidemic but confess that I help spread it. Otherwise rational, I'm a cat lover, who once kept fourteen of them. It seemed more like fourteen hundred.

This was before heightened consciousness about animal birth control. At six months old, my one male kitten turned into a female with a hyperactive sex drive. Kittens were born, and more kittens, and the kittens had kittens. I gave them to friends, anonymously and in the middle of the night, but they kept multiplying. Time has obscured the episode, but in bad dreams I still hear the pitter-patter of fifty-six feet. Since then I've confined myself to owning no more than two cats at a time, both neutered, and find two is the perfect number. They can take turns depositing hair balls on the rug, in a feline form of work-sharing, and I can whittle away at my veterinary bills. It's warming to know, as I write the checks, that the local pet hospital has a new wing and the vet's children are all happy at Harvard.

In exchange for all those checks and my devotion, I've had the unflagging contempt of my cat companions, who keep company with me while waiting for better offers. My current cat, the object of unrequited love, is a media star of sorts. The illustrator of *Cat Scan*, noted Bay Area artist Missy Dizick, likes to paint him; he's been immor-

talized in both oils and pastels. When he's not modeling, he's unemployed, other than illustrating the principle of inert matter. Said a recent lunch guest, regarding the malevolent-looking lump on the rug, "Is that thing alive?"

Previous cats had their own endearing qualities, such as the one who stuffed dead field mice, heads down and tails neatly aligned, in the squares of my latticed rubber doormat; the tomcat who sprayed on a manuscript (everyone's an editor); and the mad tabby who liked to mug the neighborhood dogs. Their owners appeared at my door carrying quivering German shepherds wrapped in blankets. "See what that damned cat of yours did this time?" I think my mistake was naming that one Cougar.

Now comes *Cat Scan* and the writings of cat lovers, cat haters and all interested parties on the subject of people and cats other than cats themselves, who, with the exception of Don Marquis' glorious Mehitabel, are rotten prose stylists. For those of us who love cats, this anthology of verse, essays, cat lore, and aphorisms will be catnip. For those who sensibly hate them, there are recipes for cooking the creatures, though for some reason, these omit the French classic, *catatouille*. Freud's casebooks don't reveal more about obsession than do Robert Byrne and Teressa Skelton, and no one draws or paints cats more delightfully than does Missy Dizick, a cat-loving wacko whose household furnishings include what she calls her "enemy chair." This is the one she never brushes. Now sagging under the weight of cat hair, it's hell on the dark suits of door-to-door salesmen.

I don't want a five-foot shelf of books on cats, but I'm devoted to this one, which culls out and collects between covers the funniest, the most affecting and the oddest that's been written on the subject. Curl up with *Cat Scan* and your favorite cat, or borrow mine. I'll miss him, but on the other hand, his litter box needs changing again.

CYRA McFADDEN

Editor's Introduction

When six Chinese accountants came to San Francisco in 1982 on an exchange visit sponsored by an American accounting firm, their hosts asked them if there was anything in particular they wanted to see. "Yes," they said through an interpreter. "We have heard that in America stores sell food for pets. We want to see if that is true." Not only do stores sell food for pets, they found out, whole supermarket aisles are devoted to it, the sight of which made them gape in amazement. In China, dogs and cats are lucky to get table scraps; yet here was a nation diverting a substantial part of its food supply to the damned things. Truly, Americans are an alien and inscrutable people. Generous to a fault.

Those six Chinese accountants didn't know the half of it. They didn't even know 1 percent. Their hosts could have killed them with culture shock, actually put them in their graves, by introducing them to such California excesses as cat psychics, cat acting coaches, cat acupuncturists, and cat pimps. I will stick to cats, the subject of this book, and forget dogs, goldfish, hamsters, parrots, and all the other blameless creatures that find themselves in ever-greater numbers spending their lives with Americans. Spreading inward across the nation from both coasts are cat motels, rent-a-cat agencies, cat retirement homes, and meowing contests. Something is spreading outward from Muncie, Indiana, as well, where cartoonist Jim Davis lives. There are now fifteen hundred different objects you can buy with pictures of Garfield on them that are hard to get off.

Cats are gaining on dogs. The American dog population seems to have stabilized at around forty-seven million, thank God, which may or may not have something to do with the jump in immigration from southeast Asia, where dog is considered a good, though not a great, entree. Cats are up to between twenty-five and thirty-five million. One home in four is now owned, in a sense, by a cat, a rise of 55 percent in the last ten years.

It gets worse. Americans paid $200 million last year for kitty litter. Cat food is on the verge of overtaking baby food in both sales and taste. The ominous fact is that American babies are decreasing slightly in numbers while cats are going up. Projecting current trends reveals that in only twenty-nine years cats will have replaced babies completely and the United States as we know it will be terminal. Imagine the gladness that will spring up in the hearts of our implacable foes in the Kremlin, not to mention the six Chinese accountants. Capitalism defeated by the common cat! Buried under a mountain of kitty litter and Meow Mix! It would be enough to make even Karl Marx, not the most bubbly personality, chuckle.

These vast historical currents can be monitored in the pages of *Cats* and *Cat Fancy*, two slick-paper monthlies that are racing to see which can first reach a circulation of one hundred thousand. According to Raymond D. Smith, publisher of *Cats*, his readers have 2.8 people and

8.55 cats per family and 5 percent of them take no other magazine. Cat shows are more popular than ever before in history, he reports, 306 having been held between May and December of 1982 compared to 288 in the same period of the previous year. "Things will be bright for cats in 1983," he predicted correctly last February in a column flanked by ads for the Flexport Intrusion Molded Oval Door, Dr. Hanson's Bullseye Pill Gun, marble gravestones from the Remembered Friend Memorials company, and Keipper's All-Wire Collapsible Coops.

Not even Raymond D. Smith, as perceptive as he is, has noticed the connection between the Black Death of the Middle Ages and Martina Navratilova's loss in the 1982 United States Open Tennis Tournament. In medieval times, cats became identified with witchcraft and the devil and were relentlessly persecuted by all right-thinking Europeans. Pope Innocent VIII in 1484 went so far as to declare official war on cats. What particularly bugged Innocent was a German cult that worshipped a goddess whose chariot was drawn by two black cats. But cats were in hot water long before that; for hundreds of years they had been subjected to insults of such a dreadful nature that even today hardened ailurophobes blanch at the details. Cats were stoned, lanced, hurled from towers, and fed to flames all over the continent. Europe was so stripped of cats that when Asiatic black rats arrived from the Holy Land in the baggage of the Crusaders they must have thought they had died and gone to heaven. They multiplied dizzily, stuffed themselves on the crops of every nation, and attacked children on streets and babies in cradles. They also played host to typhus-carrying fleas, and when the inevitable plague broke out it was appalling. Between 1334 and 1354, the Black Death killed three out of every four Europeans.

By Innocent's time, fortunately, it had become clear to a good many people that there had been a regrettable misplacement of emphasis. Rats, not cats, were the problem. Compared to rats, cats were almost a treat. A massive shift in sentiment took place. Innocent's war cry was greeted tepidly, if at all, and the cat came back in time to save Western Civilization. Cats and the one in four Europeans who were left got busy and before long there were even more cats and Europeans than there were before. People liked cats again, though it was a long time before they were seen primarily as pets rather than pesticides.

The adoption of the cat by the urban masses had to wait for the end of World War II and a key scientific advance: the creation of synthetic kitty litter. The ready availability of litter at affordable prices started a silent and continuing stampede of cats into the dwelling units of America; it is an invasion that matches in grandeur the one mounted earlier by the rats from the Holy Land. Once again, there are public health considerations. Cats, it turns out, carry toxoplasmosis.

Toxoplasmosis is more like the flu than the Black Death, but it can be dangerous, particularly for people still *in utero*. Toxoplasmosis is what Navratilova had when she was upset at the U.S. Open. *That's* the connection she has with the Black Death. One disease results from too few cats, the other from too many.

Yes, these are tough times for cat haters. Even the indifferent are feeling stabs of irritation and dismay; cats have captured such a large part of American culture they can't be avoided. The musical *Cats*, based on poems by T. S. Eliot, is a big hit in New York and *Playbill*, the magazine that is handed out at the door to all New York theatergoers, now carries ads from Ralston Purina. Walk into a bookstore looking for the Bible in jive or a concordance to the works of Danielle Steel and you will be assaulted by cat books. The books on cooking, women's studies, and nuclear war have been moved to the rear. If you've just been mugged and have only pocket change, you can buy a cat calendar, a cat decal, or a cat note pad.

You might need a cat bookmark for the paperback you already have on astrology for cats.

At least a hundred books on cats have been published in the United States in the last three years, and the fact that some of them are devoted to uses for dead ones doesn't help much. Cat titles in tiny type run page after page in the reference work *Books in Print*. The Cat Book Center in New Rochelle, New York, puts out a catalog listing 593 cat books available by mail, and that doesn't include juveniles; the juvenile catalog is due in 1984 and will list 500 titles. The public library in Glendale, California, stocks 1,400 cat books and 18,000 related pieces of printed matter and is the world's leading repository of cat literature, having recently passed Yale. There is a cat book *about* cat books, Claire Necker's *Four Centuries of Cat Books, 1570–1970*, a bibliography with some 3,200 entries.

Can you blame professional authors for feeling that the only way to survive is to write a cat book? In 1982, the Garfield books accounted for a third of all sales for trade paperbacks on the *New York Times* best-seller lists. They trivialize cats, in the opinion of Raymond D. Smith. "They aren't cat books at all," he said in a recent column. "They're comic books about a youngster dressed up in a cat costume." Jim Davis agrees. Whatever they are, they sell like mad. Smith went on to mention some *real* cat books, the kind quoted in the pages that follow.

Sure, a lot of dreck and shlock have been published about cats, but a tremendous amount of good stuff has been, too, as you are about to discover. I speak as one who has just emerged from total immersion in the great river of cat literature that flows through the centuries. The wit, insight, and variety of expression that a ten-pound animal has drawn out of writers is fantastic.

As part of the campaign for truth in publishing, I want to confess that I began life as a cat hater. They gave me asthma, so I hated them. That they may not have done it on purpose made no difference. Tests showed that raisins, ragweed, and alfalfa also gave me asthma, and so I hated them, too, and still do. On cats, though, I've come around.

Though I outgrew my allergies, I hated cats through high school, college, and eighteen years of a catless marriage. I liked dogs. If I was going to do favors for something, I wanted it to be sloppily grateful. My attitude didn't begin to change until I was ... well, catapulted into the singles jungle. I discovered that a substantial fraction of the unmarried females in my environs owned cats, petted them, hugged them, loved them, and fed them. Instead of me. Several years of hanging around places where cats lived brought me new understanding. What started out as hatred changed to envy, then to grudging admiration, and finally to what I feel about them today, which is almost affection. They *are* fascinating little critters. I salute their grace, their silky softness, and the well-oiled, slinky way they move. I marvel at their quickness, coordination, and astounding leaps. At last I see the charm of their insouciance and serenity.

An historic first occurred half-way through the compilation of this book. I fed a cat. More precisely, I gave a wary stray a saucer of milk. I sat a short distance away and watched him daintily drink it. When he was finished he raised his head and we gazed at each other. We both thought about the long relationship between our two proud species, and then we both opened our mouths and said together: "Maybe you aren't so bad after all."

ROBERT BYRNE
SAN RAFAEL, CALIFORNIA

Researcher's Counter-Introduction

The Editor is proud of waking up to something that thirty million of his more aware countrymen have known all along: Cats are superb entertainment and superior pets. Now he appears to expect some form of adulation for his "almost affection" and for prying himself loose from one crummy saucer of milk.

He deserves some credit, though, for finally admitting his error about cats...in spite of the way he goes about it. (I mean, really, trying to pin the old asthma rap on some poor long-dead pussy.)

He seems irked that our cats might be better fed than the cats of Chinese accountants, or even than the accountants themselves. Do you get the feeling that deep down Byrne still feels that cats *should* live on table droppings? Notice the term "excesses" he applies to his list of helpful cat professionals and services and the way he runs on about toxoplasmosis and Innocent's war. Was it necessary to *list* the various tortures?

It makes a cat lover wonder. I wonder about the Editor's motives for his alleged change of heart. He admits women have played an important role in his new estimation of cats. He apparently thinks that purring over kitties might induce their mistresses to do some purring over him. I would caution Byrne. Women, like cats, are quick to detect insincerity. Hollowness of tone in the praise of feline virtue is tolerated neither by us *real* cat people nor the objects of our passion.

But if he really *has* come around with regard to cats, good for him.

TERESSA A. SKELTON
SAN FRANCISCO, CALIFORNIA

Love & Hate

Cat lovers can readily be identified. Their clothes always look old and well used. Their sheets look like bath towels and their bath towels look like a collection of knitting mistakes.

> Eric Gurney
> *How to Live with a Calculating Cat*

With their qualities of cleanliness, discretion, affection, patience, dignity, and courage, how many of us, I ask you, would be capable of being cats?

> Fernand Méry
> *Her Majesty the Cat*

I love cats because I love my home, and little by little they become its visible soul. A kind of active silence emanates from these furry beasts who appear deaf to orders, to appeals, to reproaches, and who move in a completely royal authority through the network of our acts, retaining only those that intrigue or comfort them.

> Jean Cocteau (1889–1963)

In its flawless grace and superior self-sufficiency I have seen a symbol of the perfect beauty and bland impersonality of the universe itself, objectively considered, and in its air of silent mystery there resides for me all the wonder and fascination of the unknown.

> H. P. Lovecraft (1890–1937)

I love cats. I even think we have one at home.

> Edward L. Burlingame
> quoted by Larry Ashmead in
> *The Cat's Pajamas*

Twenty-seven cats at one time hints at monomania, but in my case it was simpler. If you like cats and have some, you get kittens; and if you like kittens and enjoy having them about, they grow up and you get more cats.

Paul Gallico (1897–1976)
Honorable Cat

Upon Death

It is to François Augustin Paradis de Moncrif that we owe the story of Mlle du Puy's music-loving cat, who listened with critical attention when his mistress played upon the harp; manifesting his pleasure if she played well and his annoyance if she blundered. Mlle du Puy attributed her skill as a harpist mainly to this cat's taste and judgment; and to mark her gratitude for so great a service she bequeathed him at her death a town house, a country house, and an income sufficient to maintain both establishments. Her family, grasping and avaricious as are most kith and kin, contested the will and succeeded, after a long struggle in the courts, in wrestling from the legatee an estate which, by every law of justice and morality, was his and his alone.

Agnes Repplier (1855–1950)
The Fireside Sphinx

Mlle du Puy inserted this clause in her will: "Item: I desire my sister, Marie Bluteau, and my niece, Madame Calonge, to look to my cats. If both cats should survive me, thirty sous a week must be laid out upon them, in order that they may live well. They are to be served daily, in a clean and proper manner, with two meals of meat soup, the same as we eat ourselves, but it is to be given them separately in two soup plates. The bread is not to be cut up into the soup, but must be broken into squares about the size of a nut, otherwise they will refuse to eat it. A ration of meat, finely minced, is to be added to it; the whole is then to be mildly seasoned, put into a clean pan, covered close, and carefully simmered before it is dished up. If only one cat should survive, half the sum mentioned will suffice." . . .

An unnamed man left his property to endow a cat hospital in which an accordion "was to be played in the auditorium by one of the regular nurses, to be selected for that purpose exclusively, the playing to be kept up for ever and ever, without cessation day and night, in order that the cats may have the privilege of always hearing and enjoying that instrument which is the nearest approach to the human voice." . . .

A Buddhist foundation, Jikeiin, operates a cemetary in Tokyo that will cremate your cat or dog on its death. For ten dollars a year, the pet's ashes are preserved until your own death, when you and your cat are interred together forever in Tama Dog and Cat Memorial Park (the bill for which is a prepaid $3,350).

Leonore Fleischer
The Cat's Pajamas

When Dr. William Grier died in 1963 in San Diego, he left his entire estate of $415,000 to his two cats. When the cats died two years later, the money went to George Washington University.

The Guinness Book of World Records

The white tower had been built by Mary in an effort to get the thirty cats out of the house, and to provide Ernest with a place more becoming to work in than his bedroom. It worked with the cats but not with Ernest. The ground floor of the tower was the cats' quarters, with special sleeping, eating and maternity accommodations, and they all lived there with the exception of a few favorites like Crazy Christian, Friendless Brother and Ecstasy, who were allowed house privileges.

A. E. Hotchner
Papa Hemingway

I never shall forget the indulgence with which he treated Hodge, his cat, for whom he himself used to go out and buy oysters, lest the servants having that trouble should take a dislike to the poor creature. I am, unluckily, one of those who have an antipathy to a cat, so that I am uneasy when in the room with one; and I own, I frequently suffered a good deal from the presence of the same Hodge. I recollect him one day scrambling up Dr. Johnson's breast, apparently with much satisfaction, while my friend, smiling and half-whistling, rubbed down his back, and pulled him by the tail; and when I observed he was a fine cat, [he said] "Why, yes, Sir, but I have had cats whom I liked better than this"; and then, as if perceiving Hodge to be out of countenance, adding, "but he is a very fine cat, a very fine cat indeed."

James Boswell
The Life of Samuel Johnson

An ordinary cat will devote a whole day to the circumvention of the lodger's canary, rather than spend an hour on the landlady's rats. A single bullfinch in the drawing-room is worth a wilderness of mice in the pantry.

Louis Robinson
Wild Traits in Tame Animals

There was a radio program in Great Britain on which celebrities told what they'd take to a desert island if they were cast away. Christopher Milne (the original Christopher Robin of *Winnie the Pooh* fame) declared that he would take a pregnant cat. . . .

Colette, author of *Gigi* and the *Claudine* novels, was a celebrated cat lover. On a visit to New York she spied a cat sitting in the street. At once she went over to talk to it, and the two of them mewed at each other for a friendly minute. Colette turned to her companion and said, with a heartfelt smile, "Enfin! Quelqu'un qui parle francais!" (Finally! Someone who speaks French!)

Leonore Fleischer
The Cat's Pajamas

Be-*oooo*tiful cat! Delicious cat! Exquisite cat! Satiny cat! Cat like a soft owl, cat with paws like moths, jewelled cat, miraculous cat! Cat, cat, cat, cat.

Doris Lessing
Particularly Cats

I suspect that many an ailurophobe hates cats only because he feels they are better than he is—more honest, more secure, more loved, more whatever he is not.

Winifred Carriere

Ailurophiles and Ailurophobes
by Paul Gallico (1897–1976)

One could, I suppose, arbitrarily divide the peoples of the world into two classifications, the ailurophiles and the ailurophobes, from the Greek, the philes being lovers of cats, the phobes those who hate or fear them.

There is a whole library of research on the phobia of those who cannot bear the cat and these fall into groups themselves: people who cannot endure them for psychological reasons having to do with their own natures; those who are subject to atavistic tremors in the face of this animal; and those who are definitely physically affected by their presence and react with disgust to the point of nausea or break out into allergic rashes.

But I have never seen a single line to explain why it is that puss loves them one and all and if there is a phobe in the room will make a beeline for the party, purr, roll over, flatter, cajole, and jump up onto the victim's lap murmuring endearments.

Toward us philes who have the warmest affection for kitty on various levels and for many diverse reasons ranging from amused delight to love, the cat is able to show the utmost indifference. To an outpouring of fondness on our part, demonstrated by stroking it, scratching it, hugging it to us and crooning over it, cat will yawn and, as soon as our smothering hold upon it is released, get up, jump down, and go. This is understandable. Amorousness can be cloying and disagreeable, particularly if practiced at the wrong moment.

...I have always thought I understood my cat's attitudes toward my overreacting to it and respected it.

But what about the poor phobes? It would be simple to say that, feeling rejected, the animal is determined to win over such a one just to show that it can be done. But that isn't a cat. That's more a dog's characteristic. Cat simply doesn't care.

And besides, it is impossible. It isn't going to work ever. The phobe is not to be reformed by such flattery. The presence of a cat fills him with whatever you care to ascribe to the Greek root—fear, dread, horror, bad memories ... and nothing is going to cure them.

Felis domestica most certainly would have found this out in its three- or four-thousand-year association with human beings.

Well then, to return to the mystery, what is it? A gag, a perverted sense of humor? Or, even, pity and compassion for someone who through an illness is missing something in life? I wouldn't put anything past a cat.

Or if it were a kind of vengeance, a deliberate decision to increase the discomfort of the sufferer, it would not surprise me. If the cat on the one hand was deified and pampered, it has also been greatly sinned against, and the history of its treatment down through the ages at the hand of humans, as we know, shows the balance to be all against us. Is there some ratiocination in whatever may be the mental processes of kitty that works out to, "Hullo, I scent a prospect who, for one reason or another, cannot bear me. Whoopee! Here's where I really spoil his day and chalk up one for our side."

Or is it the powerful attraction of unlikes, the two opposite poles of the magnets that leap to be joined together; the love-hate dependency which is perhaps the basis of most relationships, human or animal? Is love only truly to be distinguished by suffering and torment, and are the cats and their phobes the only true lovers, and we philes but a pale reflection?

I have another suggestion: Is it the syndrome of the lady who is convinced that she is the only one who can reform the hardened or habitual drunk or wean the unhappy homosexual away from his affliction, even though, with but the scantiest of exceptions, it has never been done?

And yet they will go on trying to do it. Is this cat's attempted seduction then, this irresistible challenge to accomplish the impossible, based on arrogance or the mathematics of chance that it will be the one to achieve the never-before-accomplished?

Well, this is certainly a human trait and I suppose we owe progress to it. And since in one way or another, all human traits are derived from our ancestors in the animal kingdom, it might not be too farfetched to suggest that puss feels the same stirring of the pioneer spirit.

from *Honorable Cat*

Animals have these advantages over man: they never hear the clock strike, they die without any idea of death, they have no theologians to instruct them, their last moments are not disturbed by unwelcome and unpleasant ceremonies, and no one starts lawsuits over their Wills. Animals hear about death for the first time when they die.

Arthur Schopenhauer (1788–1860)
Essays

I think I could turn and live with animals,
They are so placid and self-contained,
I stand and look at them long and long.
They do not sweat and whine about their condition,
They do not lie awake in the dark and weep for their
    sins,
They do not make me sick discussing their duty to
    God . . .

Walt Whitman (1819–1892)
from "Song of Myself"

Five Famous Cat Lovers

MOHAMMED (570–632)
The founder of the Muslim faith approved of cats but felt dogs were unclean. He once cut off a sleeve in order not to disturb his sleeping cat.

PETRARCH (1304–1374)
When the poet died his cat was put to death and mummified.

CARDINAL RICHELIEU (1585–1642)
This Prince of the Church reserved one of his rooms for cats, where overseers fed them chicken pâtés twice a day. When he died the overseers and cats were provided for.

SIR WINSTON CHURCHILL (1874–1965)
The statesman enjoyed eating with his ginger kitten, Jock. Servants were often sent to find the pet so meals could begin.

ALBERT SCHWEITZER (1875–1965)
Although left-handed, Dr. Schweitzer would often write prescriptions with his right hand because his cat Sizi liked to sleep on his left arm and could not be disturbed.

Five Famous Cat Haters

HENRY III (1551–1589)
Henry was like a lion when persecuting the Protestant minority in France, but the presence of a cat turned him into a chicken. He would faint if a cat came close.

GEORGES LOUIS LECLERC DE BUFFON (1707–1788)

The French naturalist praised dogs, but claimed that cats possessed "an innate malice and perverse disposition which increases as they grow up." He added that they "easily assume the habits of society but never acquire its manners."

NOAH WEBSTER (1758–1843)

In his dictionary, Webster had little good to say about cats. According to him, the cat is "a deceitful animal and when enraged extremely spiteful."

JOHANNES BRAHMS (1833–1897)

Brahms spent much of his time at the window trying to hit neighborhood cats with a bow and arrow, a sport at which he became quite adept.

DWIGHT D. EISENHOWER (1890–1969)

The president not only kept a shotgun next to his television set for shooting crows at his home in Gettysburg, he also ordered that any cat seen on the grounds should be shot.

adapted from *The Book of Lists #2*

There does not live a man in the world who so greatly hates cats, so deeply hates them. I hate their eyes, their face, their gaze.

Ronsard (1524–1585)

God save all here, barring the cat.

Irish toast

The cat appears to have feelings only for himself, loves only conditionally, and enters into relations with people only to abuse them.

Georges Louis Leclerc de Buffon (1707–1788)

In 1888, a bumbling farmer dug up an ancient Egyptian cat necropolis at Beni Hasan. The cemetary contained thousands of mummified cats that had been interred, sometimes with embalmed mice for afterworld meals. Enterprising workers unwrapped the cats and sent a consignment of nineteen tons of bones to England for use as fertilizer.

Time
December 7, 1981

Cat house—A disorderly house; e.g., any building where cats are raised.

Raymond D. Smith
Cats magazine
November 1982

Our English word for cat-hater, ailurophobe, is confusing; it is based on the belief that the mouse-killer mentioned in ancient Greek writings was a cat, but we now know that it was some member of the weasel family, probably the marten or polecat.

William H. A. Carr
The Basic Book of the Cat

A Dithyramb on Cats
by Orlando Dobbin

> Confound the cats! All cats—always—
> Cats of all colours, black, white, grey;
> By night a nuisance and by day—
> Confound the cats!

Ignorant people think it's the noise which fighting cats make that is so aggravating, but it ain't so; it's the disgusting grammar they use.

Mark Twain (1835–1910)

Something is going on right now in Mexico that I happen to think is cruelty to animals. I refer, of course, to cat juggling.

Steve Martin

Wanted
by Shel Silverstein

> Can anyone lend me two twelve-pound rats?
> I want to rid my house of cats.

The great charm of cats is their rampant egotism, their devil-may-care attitude toward responsibility, their disinclination to earn an honest dollar. In a continent which screams neurotically about cooperation and The Golden Rule, cats are disdainful of everything but their own immediate interests, and they contrive to be so suave and delightful about it that they even receive the apotheosis of a National Week.

Robertson Davies
The Table Talk of Samuel Marchbanks

The Cat
by Ogden Nash

> You get a wife, you get a house,
> Eventually you get a mouse.
> You get some words regarding mice,
> You get a kitty in a trice.
> By two A.M. or thereabout,
> The mouse is in, the cat is out.
> It dawns upon you, in your cot,
> The mouse is silent, the cat is not.
> Instead of Pussy, says your spouse,
> You should have bought another mouse.

from *Many Long Years Ago*

I could half persuade myself that the word felonious is derived from the feline temper.

> Robert Southey (1774–1843)
> in a letter to his daughter, 1824
> (for full letter, see page 137)

A cat is a soft, indestructible automaton provided by nature to be kicked when things go wrong in the domestic circle.

> Ambrose Bierce (1842–1914)
> *The Devil's Dictionary*

Favorite Cat Recipes

CAT NIP

1 oz. 140-proof rum
4 oz. pineapple juice, unsweetened
2 oz. heavy cream
2 oz. cat

Place ingredients in blender. Fill with ice cubes. Blend at high speed for 30 seconds.

Pour into 8-oz goblet. Garnish with pineapple stick and anchovies.

CAT MOLD

1 tbsp. plain gelatin
4 tbsp. cold water
8 hard-cooked kittens
2 tsp. salt
¼ tsp. black pepper
3 tbsp. mayonnaise

Soak the gelatin in cold water and dissolve it over hot water. Put kittens through a ricer or sieve and mix well with other ingredients. Add gelatin and mix well.

Pour into 2-qt. ring mold and chill until set (about 3 to 4 hours). Unmold on large plate. Fill center with chilled tuna or cat salad.

Optional: Garnish with whole kittens in aspic.

Cat Faces

3 to 4 cat faces
raisins

On a floured pastry board roll out cat faces to about a 10-inch diameter. Try to keep edges as round as possible.

Use raisins to spell out "Have a Nice Day" around bottom edge of each face.

Bake in preheated 375-deg. oven for 30 minutes or until nicely browned.

Great with a glass of milk for an after-school snack.

> *The Disgusting, Despicable Cat Cookbook*
> John P. Eaton and Julie Kurnitz

French Cuisine

Humans have sometimes eaten cats, and not just under wartime conditions. The Trobriand Islanders used to roast a galantine of cat stuffed with fat mice on ceremonial occasions. Closer to home, the French seem to have produced the largest number of bizarre cat eaters. The famous glutton of the early nineteenth century, Terrare of Versailles, liked to eat a whole raw cat, regurgitating a ball of skin and fur half an hour after his meal like a bird of prey.

> David Taylor
> *The Cat: An Owner's Maintenance Manual*

Mr. Brooks, The Piemaker

I lodged in the same house with a pieman once, sir, and a very nice man he was—reg'lar clever chap, too—make pies out o' anything, he could. "What a number o' cats you keep, Mr. Brooks," says I, when I'd got intimate with him. "Ah," says he, "I do—a good many." "You must be wery fond o' cats," says I. "Other people is," says he, a-winkin' at me; "they ain't in season till the winter, though," says he. "Not in season!" says I. "No," says he, "fruits is in, cats is out." "Why, what do you mean?" says I. "Mean?" says he. "That I'll never be a party to the combination o' the butchers, to keep up the price o' meat," says he. "Mr. Weller," says he, a-squeezing my hand wery hard, and vispering in my ear, "don't mention this here again, but it's the seasonin' as does it. They're all made o' them noble animals," says he, a-pointin' to a wery nice little tabby kitten, "and I seasons 'em for beefsteak, weal, or kidney, 'cording to the demand. And more than that," says he, "I can make a weal a beefsteak, or a beefsteak a kidney, or any one a mutton at a minute's notice, just as the market changes and appetites wary."

"He must have been a very ingenious young man," said Mr. Pickwick, with a slight shudder.

Charles Dickens (1812–1870)
The Pickwick Papers

Q. Do rabbits have claws like cats?
A. No, ma'am, they have distinctly different paws. That, in fact, is why Paris butchers always leave the paws on dressed rabbits. So shoppers—those who prefer rabbit—can buy with confidence.

L. M. Boyd
"The Grab Bag," March 12, 1983
(syndicated newspaper column)

The Edible Cat

CAT (*felis domesticus*): A carnivorous quadruped never (knowingly) eaten in the British Isles. But its flesh has been described by Englishmen who have tried it as very good. Labouchere, who ate cats during the siege of Paris in 1870, wrote that a cat was "something between a rabbit and a squirrel, with a flavor of its own. It is delicious. Don't drown your kittens, eat them."

> André Simon (1877–1970)
> *A Concise Encyclopedia of Gastronomy*
> (first published in England in 1939 by the Wine and Food Society)

Skydiving Cats and Chickens

[Editor's note: In the June 1980 edition of the magazine Flying, *contributing editor Gordon Baxter described a story he had heard about a skydiving cat on the isle of Bois Blanc in the Straits of Mackinac. It seems that a group of fun lovers there were taking a local cat on rides in a light plane and jettisoning him at an altitude of three thousand feet by sliding him out the door through a length of stovepipe. Legend had it that the cat would wait by the runway to be taken up again. Baxter asked the American Society for the Prevention of Cruelty to Animals if they knew anything about the practice and was told: "Any cat that persists in hanging around small airports and light aircraft is beyond concern of us." In the May 1982 issue, Baxter reviewed some of the mail the article elicited; excerpts follow.]*

A pilot from Long Island reported that he had heard a seat belt dangling outside his 1952 Piper Pacer after take-off. With full flaps he slowed to about 55 mph, and when he opened the door his eight-year-old Siamese, Cognac, mysteriously appeared and sprang out of the airplane 1,100 feet off the ground. Right over the field. The pilot landed and found the cat sitting by the runway, unhurt, washing itself, licking a paw and rubbing it over its head. A $100 bet was quickly made that the pilot could drop another cat unharmed. By drop time Sunday the pilot had $1,400 out in bets and a good crowd. He dropped a gray-and-white stray from 1,200 feet, not wanting to risk Cognac again even for money. The stray sailed over the onlookers, missed them by 200 feet, got up and headed for the woods with a speed that indicated outrage but no injury. The following Sunday, however, another pilot launched two feline fatalities, "and we all felt pretty embarrassed for participating in such a stunt."

A reader from Texas sent a clipping from an April 1934 issue of *Popular Aviation* proving again that nothing was new. The cat was launched with a harness and three-foot parachute from a Curtis Robin. The chute was lost on opening, but the cat survived a free fall of 1,000 feet, "although stunned," read the official report.

A skydiving Ph.D. from California wrote about a cat whose self-righting capability proved fatal. The reluctant cat was launched in a tumble, then rolled itself into a fouled chute. The doctor's final experiment was with a large white leghorn rooster pushed out at 2,500 feet. The doc dove out to go along as observer. "He went nose down, full delta, until near the ground, then deployed his brakes and flaps, but they came unglued. He creamed in. There were still feathers in the air when I landed." The doc says he has never witnessed a successful animal jump.

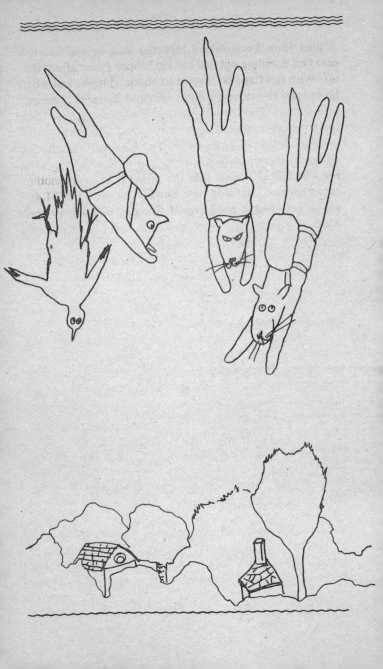

Nearly all the writers asked that their names be withheld. A staffer from ABC's "That's Incredible" called and wanted names and addresses. After watching a "60 Minutes" treatment of general aviation I decided I did not want to be remembered as the guy who started the "catapult" craze in America.

And I would warn any of you who are captivated with the idea of skydiving cats that God may be a giant Siamese.

Owning a tomcat is akin to working in some menial capacity for one of the notorious Lotharios of show business.

John D. MacDonald
The House Guests

Four by William Cole

What Could It Be?

> I really do not like that cat;
> I don't know why, it's maybe that
> She's vicious, cruel, rude, ungrateful,
> Smelly, treacherous, and hateful,
> Supercilious, stupid, eerie,
> Thoroughly boring, dull and dreary,
> Scheming, cold, and unproductive,
> Inconvenient and destructive—
> But most, I've just a *feeling* that
> I *really* do not like that cat.

Now Here's My Plan

A cat will land on its feet—
Is this really true?
Well, I live on the twentieth floor,
And I tell you what we'll do...

Way It Goes

To the pussy we're indebted
For upholstered chairs all shredded,
For that all-pervading stink
For the box beneath the sink,
For the hairs we have to pluck
From the clothes on which they're stuck,
For the horrifying sound
When the mating time comes 'round,
And—of course—what follows that—
Is (again!) a pregnant cat.
After *that* the problem bitter—
What to do with *this* damn litter!

Pussy, you're a horrid creature
With not one redeeming feature!

Deep Down

Ding dong dell
Pussy's in the well.
I think that's swell.

Some people say that cats are sneaky, evil, and cruel. True, and they have many other fine qualities as well.

Missy Dizick

If your pet rock can't care for itself, tie a cat around its neck and throw it in the river.

Karla Brown

My Wonderful Cat
by Robert Byrne

No doubt about it, my cat is the worst.
Loudly I shout it: The creature is cursed.
When dinner is cooking, he's home on the range;
When no one is looking, the food gets the mange.
He knocks over saucepans, dishes, and glasses,
He steps in the sugar, the cream, the molasses.
He gets fleas and disease,
He gets stuck up in trees,
He scratches my elbows, my hands, and my knees,
He's making me wheeze, he's making me itch,
He's making the veterinarian rich;
He's a mass of psychosis, he's got halitosis,
Rickets and crickets and toxoplasmosis;
He flies into rages, he's spiteful and petty,
He turns the sports pages into confetti.
Some of his acts have a serious nature
Worthy of Acts of the state legislature:
He scowls and he howls and he dismembers owls
And you never know where he will empty his bowels;
He jumps onto faces when people are sleeping,
Causing disgraces, hysteria, weeping,
Stresses and strife and shrieking, of course,
And now my dear wife is seeking divorce.
She's leaving my life and she's taking our brat,
Which is why I will always be fond of my cat.

Cats & Dogs

I value in the cat that independence and almost ungrateful temper which prevents it from attaching itself to any one; the indifference with which it passes from the salon to the housetop. When you caress it, it stretches itself out and arches its back, indeed; but that is caused by physical pleasure, and not, as in the case of the dog, by a silly satisfaction in loving and being faithful to a master who returns thanks in kicks. The cat lives alone, has no need of society, does not obey except when it likes, pretends to sleep that it may see the more clearly, and scratches everything that it can scratch.

François René de Chateaubriand (1768–1848)

Let us love dogs, let us love only dogs! Men and cats are unworthy creatures.

Marie Konstantinova Bashkirtsev (1860–1884)
The Journal of a Young Artist

I have always thought of a dog lover as a dog in love with another dog.

James Thurber (1894–1961)

Confront a child, a puppy, and a kitten with sudden danger; the child will turn instinctively for assistance, the puppy will grovel in abject submission to the impending visitation, the kitten will brace its tiny body for frantic resistance. . . .

Not as a bond-servant or dependent has this proudest of mammals entered the human fraternity; not as a slave like the beasts of burden, or a humble camp follower like the dog. The cat is domestic only as far as it suits its own ends; it will not be harnessed nor suffer any dictation as to its goings-out or comings-in.

> Saki (Hector Hugh Munro) (1870–1916)
> "The Achievement of the Cat"
> in *The Square Egg*

The cat, an aristocrat, merits our esteem, while the dog is only a scurvy type who got his position by low flatteries.

> Alexandre Dumas (1812–1870)

Anybody, but *anybody*, any lout, any half-wit, any scruffy, self-centered moron, can command the affection and the servile obedience of a dog, but it takes intelligence and understanding—sometimes I think a certain psychic rapport—to win the affection of a cat....

Cats cannot be drilled or regimented. Dogs, yes. One can imagine a platoon of poodles marching stiffly up and down the barrack square, and liking it. One can see them wheeling and doubling, sloping arms and presenting tails, in strict obedience to the hoarse barks of their sergeant major. Cats, never. (Is it not significant that sergeant majors invariably bark? They never mew. One who did would seldom be recommended for a commission.)

> Beverly Nichols
> *Cats' X.Y.Z.*

It is generally believed that cats cannot be taught to do tricks. That is not true. It is true, however, that cats are far more difficult to teach than dogs—not because they are less intelligent but because they are too sensible to think that sort of thing is really worthwhile.

> William H. A. Carr
> *The Basic Book of the Cat*

Dogs as a general rule tend to keep asking, "What would you advise me to do now? I just sit doing nothing. There must be something that would give me fun. Why don't you start something for me? You're a man; you must know better than I what I want to do."

Cats do not need to be shown how to have a good time, for they are unfailingly ingenious in that respect. Nor do they need to be told who is the master, for it is a matter of extreme indifference to them. They are affectionate to those whom they recognize as friends and humor others by falling in with their wishes, provided they are not too whimsical.

James Mason and Pamela Kellino
The Cats in Our Lives

The almost pathological dependency of some dogs make them ideal child substitutes. In a sense, such dogs are helping control the human population.

Michael W. Fox.
Understanding Your Cat

Nature Notes: Cats
by Louis MacNeice (1907–1964)

> Incorrigible, uncommitted,
> They leavened the long flat hours of my childhood,
> Subtle, the opposite of dogs,
> And, unlike dogs, capable
> Of flirting, falling, and yawning anywhere,
> Like women who want no contract
> But going their own way
> Make the way of their lovers lighter.
>
> from *The Collected Poems of Louis MacNeice*

If a dog jumps into your lap, it is because he is fond of you; but if a cat does the same thing, it is because your lap is warmer.

Alfred North Whitehead (1861–1947)

There are a lot of good reasons why a cat makes an ideal pet. Cats are quiet. They need very little space, a minimum of care, and they're clean. It is also cheaper to feed a cat than a St. Bernard. They are devoted, affectionate and understanding. You can tell your cat anything and he'll still love you. If you lose your job or your best friend, your cat will think no less of you. Your cat will never threaten your popularity by barking at three in the morning. He won't attack the mailman or eat the drapes, although he may climb the drapes to see how the room looks from the ceiling.

> Helen Powers
> *The Biggest Little Cat Book in the World*

A dog is prose, a cat is a poem.

> Jean Burden
> quoted in *The Cat Notebook*

The cat lets Man support her. But unlike the dog, she is no hand-licker. Furthermore, unlike Man's other great good friend, the horse, the cat is no sweating serf of Man. The only labor she condescends to perform is to catch mice and rats, and that's fun.

> Vance Packard
> *The Human Side of Animals*

> To Someone very Good and Just,
> Who has proved worthy of her
>   trust,
> A Cat will sometimes condescend—
>   The Dog is Everybody's friend.
>> Oliver Herford (1863–1935)

Cats Versus The Competition
by Paul Gallico (1897–1976)

The cat competes for the hearts and minds of people, not to mention the freeloading privileges, with the dog, the monkey, the horse, the rabbit, and a variety of small rodents and birds kept in their pockets by little boys. We'll leave out birds as being too stupid even to be handicapped in the race. Incidentally, I am given to understand by those who know that the horse also rates high in the stupidity stakes. Furthermore, although one can love one's horse or donkey, one doesn't ordinarily let it inside the house. This would seem to limit the competition to those animals admitted, by normal people, into the living room. . . .

While dogs touch me emotionally and I cannot resist their appeal, they strike me, by and large, as being witless, hysterical, and mindless creatures except when one hears of a specimen who has had the sense to yap upon noting the house is on fire, or the courage to bite the burglar in the trousers, or the intelligence to fish a child out of the water. The manner in which the dog can be conditioned has brought the name of Pavlov into the language. They can actually be trained to point out where a square meal in the shape of a succulent bird is hiding in a bush . . . instead of keeping the secret of their discovery to themselves. And after his equally dim master has caused the bird to fly up before shooting it, instead of sensibly potting it on the ground and thus making certain it gets into the oven, the dog then actually cooperates in an act of even more inexplicable stupidity: he sniffs out what ought to be a private and delectable meal for himself, takes it in his mouth, and fetches it back to the hunter. You wouldn't find any cat consenting to such lunatic behavior. This same cat will, however, often voluntarily donate a mouse to its family as an act either of love or gratitude. It is a most wondrous gift and, in my opinion, completely thought out beforehand. . . .

Dogs are dirty, monkeys are dirty . . . but the cat, by

instinct and heredity, is scrupulously clean and even the most dejected and filthy alley bum will be seen having a go every so often at washing himself, although with the condition of our city streets it is bound to be a losing game. . . .

. . . The cat likes nice smells such as flowers, spices, perfumes. It also likes nice things to lie on such as silks, satins, or furs. A healthy cat has no odor, its fur shines. It presents the appearance of a lady or a gentleman. . . .

Puss is equally far in the lead with its eating habits. The dog slurps and gobbles greedily, the monkey scatters its food all over the premises. The cat goes at its dinner quietly and tidily and what is more exhibits a trait found in neither of the others and likewise not in humans, that is, when it has had enough it stops and walks away even should there be some left in the dish. . . .

. . . There is the little matter of disposal of droppings in which the cat is far ahead of his rivals. The dog is somehow thrilled by what he or any of his friends have produced, hates to leave it, adores smelling it, and sometimes eats it. The monkey is simply disinterested and leaves it where it lies. The cat covers it up if it can. . . .

The cat . . . is not for the pompous, the conceited, the stuffed shirt, or the unmitigated tyrant. Nor is this animal too desirable for the individual with a psychic leakage, lack of self-confidence, or a bleeding inferiority complex. The former, exposed to the behavior of puss, will be permanently offended, the latter equally permanently hurt.

It is on this level of relationship to the nominal head of the house that the domesticated cat and dog differ so greatly.

The dog offers visible signs of worship at any time of

night or day. Many dog owners both need and accept this perpetual approbation as their due. The cat maintains a constant reserve and doles out its favors sparingly. This puts a greater price and value upon these favors and the cat man is therefore the more gratified and uplifted upon receipt.

The dog seems to be the natural venerator of the human species. At some stage of its development it became contented to have a bone tossed to it at the fireside. The cat has always been prepared to go out and work for its own bone.

from *Honorable Cat*

Dogs Are Not Purrfect
by Robert Stearns

It is time to settle the cat *versus* dog question once and for all. . . . There is a ridiculous idea that dogs are superior to cats because cats cannot be trained. A cat will not jump into a lake and bring back a stick; would you? A cat has a terrific sense of humor, but it sees nothing funny or cute parading in doll's clothes. A dachshund, on the other hand, is delighted to be dressed in little lederhosen and an Alpine sweater. If you want a cat to do something out of the ordinary, you must first convince it that there is a reason for the diversion, that dignity will not be sacrificed and that cooperation is to the cat's advantage. Then, the cat will gladly comply—if it feels like it.

Dogs are the first to recognize the superiority of cats. Their frustration is expressed in belligerence that often spells doom for the dog. No dog can handle a full-grown cat by itself. The cat will run, of course, but only until it decides how to dispose of the dog.

Tuffy, a cat of my acquaintance, used to handle its pursuers by leading them at top speed from broad daylight into my darkened garage. There Tuffy would immediately leap to the window sill and perch while the disoriented dog bounded off to stumble over lawn mowers, garbage cans and, on good days, straight into a brick wall.

When it comes to the advantages of cats *versus* dogs as pets, there is no competition. Try going away for a weekend, leaving your German shepherd alone with a bowl of dry food, some water, and a litter box....

Among animals, cats are the top-hatted, frock-coated statesmen going about their affairs at their own pace. Dogs are the peasants dutifully plodding behind their leaders. A human may go for a stroll with a cat; he has to walk a dog. The cat leads the way, running ahead, tail high, making sure you understand the arrangement. If you should happen to get ahead, the cat will never allow you to think it is following you. It will stop and clean some hard-to-reach spot, or investigate a suspicious movement in the grass; you will find yourself waiting and fidgeting like the lackey you are. But this is not annoying to cat lovers, who understand and appreciate a good joke, even when it is on them.

from *Cat Catalog*

Said the Cat: "We're all mad here. I'm mad. You're mad."

"How do you know I'm mad?" asked Alice.

"You must be," said the Cat, "or you wouldn't have come here."

Alice didn't think that proved it at all; however, she went on: "and how do you know that you're mad?"

"To begin with," said the Cat, "a dog's not mad. You grant that?"

"I suppose so," said Alice.

"Well then, a dog growls when it's angry and wags its tail when it's pleased. Now, *I* growl when I'm pleased and wag my tail when I'm angry. Therefore I'm mad."

Lewis Carroll (1832–1898)
Alice's Adventures in Wonderland

What stroke do cats use when they swim? The dog paddle.

David Taylor
The Cat: An Owner's Maintenance Manual

Cats make exquisite photographs. They don't keep bouncing at you to be kissed just as you get the lens adjusted.

Gladys Taber
Ladies Home Journal
October 1941

Miscellany I

The kind man feeds his beast before sitting down to dinner.

Hebrew proverb

The cat loves fish, but hates wet feet.

Medieval proverb

The cat dreams of garbage.

Hindu proverb

When I play with my cat, who knows whether she is not amusing herself with me more than I with her?

Michel de Montaigne (1533–1592)
Essays, Book II

Shakespeare (1564–1616) On Cats

My sister crying, our maid howling, our cat wringing her hands.

Two Gentlemen of Verona
act 2, scene 3, line 7

I could endure anything before but a cat, and now he's a cat to me.

All's Well That Ends Well
act 4, scene 3, line 266

The cat, with eyes of burning coal,
Now couches 'fore the mouse's hole.

Pericles, Prince of Tyre
act 3, scene 1, line 5

A cat will never drown if she sees the shore.

Francis Bacon (1561–1626)

Nothing is more playful than a young cat, nor more grave than an old one.

Thomas Fuller (1608–1661)

Ah! cats are a mysterious kind of folk. There is more passing in their minds than we are aware of. It comes no doubt from their being too familiar with warlocks and witches.

Sir Walter Scott (1771–1832)

There are cats and cats.

Denis Diderot (1713–1784)

The playful kitten with its pretty little tigerish gambole is infinitely more amusing than half the people one is obliged to live with in the world.

Lady Sydney Morgan (1783–1859)

A cat, with its phosphorescent eyes that shine like lanterns, and sparks flashing from its back, moves fearlessly through the darkness, where it meets wandering ghosts, witches, alchemists, necromancers, grave-robbers, lovers, thieves, murderers, grey-cloaked patrols, and all the obscene larvae that only emerge at night.

Théophile Gautier (1811–1872)

The cat is the only animal that accepts the comforts but rejects the bondage of domesticity.

Georges Louis Leclerc de Buffon (1707–1788)

What sort of philosophers are we who know absolutely nothing of the origin and destiny of cats?...

A kitten is so flexible that she is almost double; the hind part are equivalent to another kitten with which the forepart plays. She does not discover that her tail belongs to her until you tread on it.

Henry David Thoreau (1817–1862)

No matter how much cats fight, there always seem to be plenty of kittens.

Abraham Lincoln (1809–1865)

The behavior of men to animals and their behavior to each other bear a constant relationship.

Herbert Spencer (1820–1903)

Nothing is so difficult as to paint the cat's face, which as Moncrif justly observes bears a character of "finesse and hilarity." The lines are so delicate, the eyes so strange, the movements subject to such sudden impulses, that one should be feline oneself to portray such a subject.

Champfleury (Jules Husson) (1821–1889)

I have studied many philosophers and many cats. The wisdom of cats is infinitely superior.

Hippolyte Taine (1828–1893)

What's virtue in a man can't be virtue in a cat.

Gail Hamilton (1833–1896)

I must have a cat whom I find homeless, wandering about the court, and to whom, therefore, I am under no obligation. I have already selected a dirty little drunken wretch of a kitten to be the successor to my poor old cat.

Samuel Butler (1835–1902)

The French symbolist poet Stéphane Mallarmé (1842–1898), claimed that he was awakened one night by two cats talking outside his bedroom window. "What are you doing these days?" one cat asked, to which the reply was: "Right now I'm pretending to be the Mallarmé's cat."

Mark Twain (1835–1910) On Cats

In the great Zoological Gardens [of Marseille] we found specimens of all the animals the world produces, I think.... The boon companion of the colossal elephant was a common cat! This cat had a fashion of climbing up the elephant's hind legs and roosting on his back. She would sit up there, with her paws curved under her breast, and sleep in the sun half the afternoon. It used to annoy the elephant at first and he would reach up and take her down, but she would climb up again. She persisted until she finally conquered the elephant's prejudices, and now they are inseparable friends. The cat plays about her comrade's forefeet or his trunk often, until dogs approach, and then she goes aloft out of danger. The elephant has annihilated several dogs lately that pressed his companion too closely.

One of the most striking differences between a cat and a lie is that a cat only has nine lives.

We should be careful to get out of an experience only the wisdom that is in it and stop there; lest we be like the cat that sits down on a hot stove-lid. She will never sit down on a hot stove-lid again—and that is well; but also she will never sit down on a cold one.

If man could be crossed with a cat, it would improve man but deteriorate the cat.

A cat can be trusted to purr when she is pleased, which is more than can be said for human beings.
> William Ralph (Dean) Inge (1860–1954)
> *Rustic Moralist*

Cats are oppressed, dogs terrify them, landladies starve them, boys stone them, everybody speaks of them with contempt. If they were human beings we could talk of their oppressions with a studied violence, add our strength to theirs, even organize the oppressed and like good politicians sell our charity for power.

William Butler Yeats (1865–1939)
A Vision

[The cat Gypsy's] extraordinary size, his daring, and his utter lack of sympathy soon made him the leader—and, at the same time, the terror—of all the loose-lived cats in a wide neighborhood. He contracted no friendships and had no confidant. He seldom slept in the same place twice in succession, and though he was wanted by the police, he was not found. In appearance he did not lack distinction of an ominous sort; the slow, rhythmic, perfectly controlled mechanism of his tail, as he impressively walked abroad, was incomparably sinister.

Booth Tarkington (1869–1946)

There is, indeed, no single quality of the cat that man could not emulate to his advantage. He is clean, the cleanest, indeed, of all animals.... He is silent, entirely self-reliant, beautiful, and graceful. He makes his appearance and his life as exquisite as circumstances will permit. He is modest, he is urbane, he is dignified. A well-bred cat never argues. He goes about doing what he likes in a well-bred, superior manner. If he is interrupted he will look at you in mild surprise or silent reproach but he will return to his desire. If he is prevented, he will wait for a more favorable occasion. But like all well-bred individualists, the cat seldom interferes with other people's rights. His intelligence keeps him from doing many of the fool things that complicate life. Cats never write operas and they never attend them. They never sign papers, or pay taxes, or vote for president. An injunction will have no power whatever over a cat. A cat, of course, would not only refuse to obey any amendment whatever to any constitution, he would refuse to obey the constitution itself.

Carl Van Vechten (1880–1964)
The Tiger in the House

I want to create a cat like the real cats I see crossing the streets, not like those you see in houses. They have nothing in common. The cat of the streets has bristling fur. It runs like a fiend, and if it looks at you, you think it is going to jump in your face.

Pablo Picasso (1881–1973)

Cocteau (1889–1967) did not fail to observe his cats. He noticed that the white cat refused to eat if she is watched; that the doyenne only ate in the presence of the Blue Persian, but that she always refused to eat from any dish other than her own; that the son of the Siamese demanded to be fed by hand, and that the Siamese mother preferred to live in Paris rather than Milly-la-Foret, which bored her.

Fernand Méry
The Life, History and Magic of the Cat

If you want to be a psychological novelist and write about human beings, the best thing you can do is keep a pair of cats. . . .

No man has ever dared to manifest his boredom so insolently as does the Siamese tomcat when he yawns in the face of his amorously importunate wife. No man has ever dared to proclaim his illicit amours so frankly as this same tom caterwauling on the tiles.

Aldous Huxley (1894–1963)
"Sermons in Cats" in *Collected Essays*

Perhaps a child, like a cat, is so much inside of himself that he does not see himself in the mirror.

Anaïs Nin (1903–1977)
The Diary of Anaïs Nin, Vol II

All of [Nitchevo, the cat's] movements were slow and without agitation. They were accomplished with a consummate grace. Her amber eyes regarded each object with unblinking serenity. Even about food she made no haste. Each evening Lucio brought home a pint of milk for her supper and breakfast; Nitchevo sat quietly waiting on her haunches while he poured it.... Nitchevo came slowly forward to the pale blue saucer. She looked up at him once—slowly—with her unflickering yellow eyes before she started to eat, and then she gracefully lowered her small chin to the saucer's edge, the red satin tip of tongue protruding, and the room was filled with the sweet, faint music of her gently lapping.

Tennessee Williams (1914–1983)
The Malediction

"Oh, Auntie, isn't he a beauty! And is he a gentleman or a lady?"

"Neither, my dear! I had him fixed. It saves him from so many undesirable associations."

D. H. Lawrence (1885–1930)
Puss-Puss

[The cat] allowed itself to be caressed as if it were a disdainful divinity. [He] thought, as he smoothed the cat's black coat, that his contact was an illusion and that the two beings, man and cat, were as good as separated by a glass, for man lives in time, in succession, while the magical animal lives in the present, in the eternity of the instant.

> Jorge Luis Borges
> "The South" in *Ficciones*

People with insufficient personalities are fond of cats. They like being ignored.

> Henry Morgan

The human race may be divided into people who love cats and people who hate them; the neutrals being few in numbers, and, for intellectual and moral reasons, not worth considering.

> Ascribed to "an acute thinker"
> by Agnes Repplier (1855–1950)
> *The Fireside Sphinx*

A cat can climb down from a tree without the assistance of the fire department or any other agency. The proof is that no one has ever seen a cat skeleton in a tree.

> Unknown

Advertisement

Cat seeks post as companion. Interferes with everything. Interrupts everything. Most conscientious.

> quoted by Elizabeth Hamilton in
> *Cats—A Celebration*

Tuna Cookies

If you've been stumped as to what to give your cat for Christmas, consider the Catnip Christmas Cookie gift, which includes a cookie cutter in the shape of a mouse, a recipe for three dozen tuna-flavored cookies, and a card, if you have a cat that reads. Cost is $3.50. Available from Diebold Designs, Box 236, Lyme NH 03768.

from *PURRRRR! The Newsletter for Cat Lovers*
December 1982/January 1983

Advice From A Vet of the Future
(If Present Trends Continue)
by Robert Byrne

Q. How will a diet affect my cat?

A. I gather that you are not now the correct weight for your height. Dieting will make Puss happier because it will give her another warm place to nap. Skinny people have laps that are boney and uncomfortable, while fat people have no laps at all.

Q. I entertain a lot. My cat *Jaws IX* greets arriving guests by sinking her teeth deeply into their calves. What should I do? I love some of my friends almost as much as *Jaws IX*.

A. Surprised you have to ask. Your pet is trying to tell you something. Gradually reduce your entertaining to zero. Don't stop all at once, though, as sudden changes have been known to make cats cranky.

Q. My cat sprays the baby's toys.

A. Check the yellow pages for foster homes and adoption agencies. Get that kid out of the house and fast.

Q. Is it okay for a cat to sleep in the same room with a baby?

A. I don't advise it. Babies are clumsy and don't have a clear idea of what is going on. Fat ones have been known to roll over in their sleep and crush cats. While it has never been observed, it is said that babies will sometimes clamp their mouths over a cat's face and suck its breath out. If it is absolutely necessary for baby and Puss to share a room, I would suggest keeping baby under some sort of restraint.

Q. What's the best way to introduce a cat to a baby?

A. Mr. (or Ms.) Puss, I'd like you to meet Mr. (or Ms.) Baby. Don't use the cat's first name unless you also use the baby's.

Q. We are travelling with our cat to Hawaii. Should we feed him before getting on the plane?

A. No, because it would spoil his appetite. After the movie, the stewardesses will come around with trays of food for everybody. It will be embarrassing if your cat just sits there and picks at it.

Q. Would neutering make my cat happier?

A. Yes. Cats hate an owner who brings a steady procession of strangers to the house for overnight visits and who

keeps disappearing for weekends, much preferring a placid owner who sticks close to home. Neutering will help settle you down. Your pet will love you for it.

Q. What's the best way to provide for my cat after my death?

A. It depends on how old Puss is. Cats live to be about seventeen, on the average. If your cat is thirteen, put out enough food and water for four years.

Q. Since acquiring Pussy-Poo we've been having trouble with Bruno, our 200-pound German Oafhound. Whenever he sees anybody petting the cat he bursts into tears and "accidentally" knocks over the dining-room table. If Bruno turns vicious, we've had it. As a puppy he once ate a mailman.

A. Now you know why long ago I decided to specialize in cats. I think it's time to put old Bruno out to pasture. Enclosed is a list of pastures in your area.

Q. Something is seriously wrong with my cat, as you can see from the photo. I'm on the left. Should I call a priest?

A. Something is seriously wrong, all right, but not with your cat. Sitting on your sofa, unless I miss my guess, is not a cat at all, but some sort of pony or small horse. You don't need a priest, you need a jockey. Or are you pulling my leg? Everybody here at the office got a big kick out of the photo. You are so sad and the horse is so happy!

Q. I'm so mad I could spit. To save money I've been feeding my husband cat food and now all he wants to do evenings is sit on the mantle and lick himself. If I go away for a weekend he pulls down the drapes. Since I got the idea from your column, can I sue you for all you've got, or at least a comfortable sum?

A. No.

Q. Wow, cats multiply in a hurry, don't they? When I divorced my husband two years ago he gave me the cat, which I didn't know was pregnant. There are over two hundred cats around here now and the house is a living hair-ball. The neighbors call it a nightmare, the city calls it cruelty to animals, my son the engineer calls it geometric progression, and I call it quits. What do you call it?

A. Revenge.

Recently we were discussing the possibility of making one of our cats Pope, and we decided that the fact that she was not Italian, and was female, made the third point, that she was a cat, irrelevant.

Katharine Whitehorn
Leicester University Magazine
January 1965

The Impossible Dream
by Robert Byrne

> Said a jockey named Tad from Seattle
> To a cat that he rode with a saddle:
> "You'll run in horse races
> And win in some cases
> Or Tad'll skedaddle on a cat that'll."

I will admit to feeling exceedingly proud when any cat has singled me out for notice; for, of course, every cat is really the most beautiful woman in the room. That is part of their deadly fascination.

E. V. Lucas (1868–1938)
365 Days and One More

Certain Cats

Eponine, The Dinner Guest

At the first stroke of the bell she would appear, and when I came into the dining-room she would be at her post, upright on her chair, her forepaws on the edge of the tablecloth; and she would present her smooth forehead to be kissed like a well-bred little girl who was affectionately polite to relatives and old people. Her place was laid without a knife and fork, but with a glass, and she went regularly through dinner, from soup to desert, awaiting her turn to be helped, and behaving with a quiet propriety which most children might imitate with advantage.

Théophile Gautier (1811–1872)
La Ménagerie Intime

Cats can be very funny, and have the oddest ways of showing they're glad to see you. Rudimac always peed in our shoes.

W. H. Auden (1907–1973)

I have as a companion a big, greyish-red cat, very gentle like its late master. It was born in the Vatican. [Pope] Leo XII brought it up in the folds of his robes, where I had often looked at it enviously when the Pontiff gave me an audience. It was called "the Pope's cat." In that capacity it used to enjoy the special consideration of the pious. I am trying to make it forget exile, the Sistine Chapel, and the sun on Michelangelo's cupola, where it used to walk far above the earth.

François René de Chateaubriand (1768–1848)

It is difficult to obtain the friendship of a cat. It is a philosophic animal, strange, holding to its habits, friend of order and cleanliness and one that does not place its affections thoughtlessly. It wishes only to be your friend (if you are worthy) and not your slave. It retains its free will and will do nothing for that it considers unreasonable.

Seraphita remained for long hours immobile on a cushion, not sleeping, following with her eyes with an extreme intensity of attention scenes invisible to simple mortals. Her elegance, her distinction, aroused the idea of aristocracy; within her race she was at least a duchess. She doted on perfumes; with little spasms of pleasure she bit handkerchiefs impregnated with scent, she wandered among flasks on the dressing-table, and if she had been allowed to, would willingly have worn powder.

Théophile Gautier (1811–1872)
La Ménagerie Intime

Min caught a mouse and was playing with it in the yard. It had got away from her once or twice and she had caught it again, and now it was stealing off again, as she was complacently watching it with her paws tucked under her, when her friend Riorden, a stout cock, stepped up inquisitively, looked down at the mouse with one eye, turning its head, then picked it up by the tail, gave it two or three whacks on the ground, and giving it a dexterous toss in the air, caught the mouse in its open mouth. It went, head foremost and alive, down Riorden's capacious throat in the twinkling of an eye, never again to be seen in this world; Min all the while, with paws comfortably tucked under her, looking on unconcerned. What did one mouse matter, more or less, to her?

Henry David Thoreau (1817–1862)

This animal was affectionate and winning, but maniacal and wily. She would not permit any vagaries, any deviation, she intended that one should go to bed and get up at the same time. When she was discontented, she expressed in the darkness of her look nuances of irritation that her master never mistook. If he returned before eleven o'clock at night, she was waiting for him at the door, in the entrance-hall, scratching the wood, meowing before he had entered the room. Then she would roll her languorous pupils of greeny gold, rub herself against his breeches, jump on the furniture, stand herself upright to look like a small horse rearing, and when he came near her, give him, in friendship, great blows with her head. If it were after eleven o'clock she did not go up to him, but restricted herself to getting up only when he came near her, still arching her back but not caressing him. If it were later still, she would not move and she would complain grumblingly.

> J. K. Huysmans (1848–1907)
> *Là-Bas*

I called my cat William because no shorter name fits the dignity of his character. Poor old man, he has fits now, so I call him Fitz-William.

> Josh Billings (1818–1885)

A Sampling of Cat People

BETSY VON FURSTENBERG
Trying to pimp for your cat in New York is really unbelievable. All the males are fixed. I was on the phone for hours trying to find Minou a mate.

MELANIE SCHNEIDER
[Siva and Vishnu] can open all of the doors, drawers, and closets in the house. I will be sitting in the living room

with company and suddenly underwear—socks, bras, panties, everything—will just arrive in the living room. They will answer the phone and leave it off the hook. When I am eating at the table, the cats will go into the kitchen cabinet and bring me the entire box of napkins.

C. J. SUARES

Maurice is the only cat whom I have given a name to; my first wife had a lover by the name of Maurice, and she didn't think that I knew it. We were lying in bed one morning, the kittens were in the closet and Maurice, then about five weeks old, came out and climbed onto the bed. My ex-wife said, "Why, you little guy, you're not allowed on the bed. What am I gonna call you!" And I said, "Call him Maurice; he's not allowed on the bed, either."

ELLEN SCHECTER

I don't brush Salmagundi; she can't stand having the brush forced on her. I hold the brush out and she walks back and forth underneath it.

MORT GOTTLIEB

Very often I'll read scripts stretched out on the couch, and Veronica will come and lie on my stomach facing the script. I can see her head moving left to right, looking at each line. Eventually, her head is lowered till it's at the bottom of the page. Sometimes she'll wait for me to turn the page and start again at the top, little by little working her way down. One time, after a few pages, she turned to me and shook her head.

NANCY NICHOLAS

When I walk in the door, [Blur] barks like Lassie in the old movie to tell me the little crippled boy has tipped over his wheelchair and the flames are licking at him and she will lead me to the scene of the tragedy. I follow her, and we always end up in the bathroom; of course there's never anything there. But she has a very proud look. If I lie down to read, she comes and sits between me and the book. I think cats are basically anti-intellectual: they want to come between you and the printed word.

as given in Bill Hayward's
Cat People

From *Particularly Cats*
by Doris Lessing

Remembering cats, always cats, a hundred incidents involving cats, years and years of cats...often enough I say, what nonsense that one should have all this trouble and worry on account of a small animal....

...It was enchanting, a delicate fairy-tale cat, whose Siamese genes showed in the shape of the face, ears, tail, and the subtle lines of its body. Her back was tabby: from above or the back, she was a pretty tabby kitten, in grey and cream. But her front and stomach were a smoky-gold, Siamese cream, with half-bars of black at the neck. Her face was pencilled with black, fine dark rings around the eyes, fine dark streaks on her cheeks, a tiny cream-colored nose with a pink tip, outlined in black. From the front, sitting with her slender paws straight, she was an exotically beautiful beast. She sat, a tiny thing, in the middle of a yellow carpet, surrounded by five worshippers, not at all afraid of us. Then she stalked around that floor of the house, inspecting every inch of it, climbed up on to my bed, crept under the fold of a sheet, and was at home....

. . . She would crouch and fascinate me with her eyes. I stared into them, almond-shaped in their fine outline of dark pencil, around which was a second pencilling of cream. Under each, a brush stroke of dark. Green, green eyes; but in shadow, a dark smoky gold—a dark-eyed cat. But in the light, green, a clear cool emerald. Behind the transparent globes of the eyeball, slices of veined gleaming butterfly wing. Wings like jewels—the essence of wing. . . .

The little black cat, for a variety of sad reasons, was homeless and joined our household. It would have been better for harmony if she had been a male cat. As it was, the two she-cats met as enemies, crouched watching each other for hours. . . .

She is elegant. She has a curved noble profile, like a cat on a tomb. When she sits straight, paws side by side, staring, or crouches, eyes half-masked, she is still, remote, withdrawn to some distant place inside herself. At such times she is sombre, inspires awe. And she is black, black, black. Black glossy whiskers, black lashes, not a white hair anywhere. If grey cat's designer was a master of subtlety, of loving detail, then black cat's said: I shall create a black cat, the quintessence of black cat, a cat from the underworld. . . .

Black cat was not well before her second litter. There was a large bald patch on her back, and she was thin. And she was overanxious: for the week before she did not like being left alone. . . . We were all irritable: in tension because we were not going to let her keep more than two kittens, since she was in no state to feed them. That meant we would have to kill some.

On the Sunday she started labour about ten in the morning. It was a slow exhausting business. The first kitten was born about four in the afternoon. She was tired.

There was a long interval between the expulsion of the kitten and the reflex when she turned to lick it. It was a fine kitten. But we had agreed not to look too much at the kittens, not to admire these vigorous scraps of life. At last, the second kitten. Now she was very tired, and gave her mournful Please-help-me cry. Right, we said, that's it: she can keep these two and we'll get rid of the rest. We got out a bottle of Scotch and drank a lot of it. Then the third kitten: surely, surely that was enough? The fourth, the fifth, the sixth. Poor black cat, working hard, expelling kittens, then licking, and cleaning, and tidying up—in the depths of the armchair such activity. At last she was clean, and the kittens clean and nursing. She lay stretched out, purring and magnificent.

...clever cat, beautiful cat...but it was no use, we had to get rid of four kittens.

So we did. It was horrible. Two of us went out into the long field in the dark with torches, and we dug a hole while the rain fell steadily, and we buried the four dead kittens and we swore and cursed at nature, at each other, and at life; and then we went back to the long quiet farm room where the fire burned, and there was black cat on a clean blanket, a pretty, proud cat with two kittens— civilization had triumphed again. And we look incredulously at the kittens, already so strong and standing up side by side on their back paws, their minute pink front paws kneading at their mother's side. Impossible to imagine them dead, but they had been chosen by chance and at random, and if my hand had picked them up an hour ago, descending from above, the hand of fate—then these two would now be lying under heavy wet soil in a rainy field. It was a terrible night; and we drank too much; and decided definitely that we would have black cat operated on, because really, really, it was not worth it.

And grey cat climbed on the arm of the chair, crouched there, and put down a paw to touch a kitten; and black cat lashed out with her paw; and grey cat skulked off out of the house into the rain.

Next day we all felt much better; and drove off to visit the sea, which was blue and calm, the weather having changed during the night. . . .

Kitten. A tiny lively creature in its transparent membrane, surrounded by the muck of its birth. Ten minutes later, damp but clean, already at the nipple. Ten days later, a minute scrap with soft hazy eyes, its mouth opening in a hiss of brave defiance at the enormous menace sensed bending over it. . . . a human hand touches it, the human smell envelops it, a human voice reassures it. Soon it gets out of its nest, confident that the gigantic creatures all around will do it no harm. It totters, then strolls, then runs all over the house. It squats in its earth box, licks itself, sips milk, then tackles a rabbit bone, defends it against the rest of the litter. Enchanting kitten, pretty kitten, beautiful furry babyish delicious little beast. . . .

. . . grey cat brought in several mice, which she laid out on the stone floor. I had realized by then that the mice were part of the one-upmanship, a gift; but . . . dead mice are hard to see attractively. As she brought them in, I threw them out; and she looked at me with ears laid back, eyes blazing resentment. . . .

From time to time people in the house lecture the cats: Fools, idiots, why can't you be friends? Just think what fun you are missing, think how nice it would be!

Last week I trod on grey cat's tail by mistake: she let out a squawk, and black cat leaped in for a kill: instant reflex. Grey cat had lost favour and protection, so black cat thought, and this was her moment.

I apologized to grey cat, petted them both. They accepted these attentions, watching each other all the time, and went their separate ways to their separate saucers, their separate sleeping places. . . .

. . . black cat is not interested in compliments today, she does not want to be bothered. I stroke her back; it arches slightly. She lets out half a purr, in polite acknowledgment to the alien, then gazes into the hidden world behind her yellow eyes.

Roger and Geoffrey

We have always arranged a window with cat shelves fastened to the outside of houses so the cats could come and go as they pleased. But sometimes their window would be closed. Roger soon learned to beat on the outside of the screen doors with his fists, making a racket like that off-stage thunder achieved by shaking a piece of sheet metal. For about the first six years of his life, Geoffrey took the traditional approach of sitting outside the door and bellowing for it to be opened. Sometimes they would both be out there, one thumping and one shouting. I would judge each method equally effective. . . .

In 1964 Robert Hale Limited published a suspense novel of mine entitled *The End of the Night*. As a result of a momentary attack of the quaints, the dedication reads, "To Roger and Geoffrey, who left their marks on the manuscript."

In an abashed penance, I dedicate this book [*The House Guests*] to all those doctors of veterinary medicine who, despite all the cutenesses of the pooty-tat trade, have retained a respect, liking, and consideration for animals on their own primitive terms. In these affluent days of the teeny cashmere sweaters, tiny electric blankets, pedicures, exotic diets, and dear little kitty-coffins, such gentlemen are becoming ever more rare.

John D. MacDonald
from *The House Guests*

Cat Poems

Anonymous ninth-century verse written in Gaelic by a
scribe in the German abbey of Reichenau:

Pangur Ban

I and Pangur Bán, my cat,
'Tis a like task we are at;
Hunting mice is his delight,
Hunting words I sit all night.

. . . .

Oftentimes a mouse will stray
Into the hero Pangur's way;
Oftentimes my keen thought set
Takes a meaning in its net.

'Gainst the wall he sets his eye
Full and fierce and sharp and sly;
'Gainst the wall of knowledge I
All my little wisdom try.

When a mouse darts from its den,
O how glad is Pangur then!
O what gladness do I prove
When I solve the doubts I love.

So in peace our tasks we ply,
Pangur Bán, my cat, and I;
In our arts we find our bliss,
I have mine and he has his.

Practice every day has made
Pangur perfect in his trade;

I get wisdom day and night,
Turning darkness into light.

Translated by Robin Flower

Think of her beautiful gliding form,
Her tread that would scarcely crush a worm,
And her soothing song by the winter fire,
Soft as the dying throb of a lyre.

William Wordsworth (1770–1850)

The Kitten and Falling Leaves
by William Wordsworth

See the Kitten on the wall,
Sporting with the leaves that fall,
. . . .
—But the Kitten, how she starts,
Crouches, stretches, paws, and darts!
First at one, and then its fellow
Just as light and just as yellow.
There are many now—now one—
Now they stop and there are none:
What intenseness of desire
In her upward eye of fire!
With a tiger-leap half-way
Now she meets the coming prey,
Lets it go as fast, and then
Has it in her power again:
Now she works with three or four,
Like an Indian conjurer;
Quick as he in feats of art,

Far beyond in joy of heart.
Were her antics played in the eye
Of a thousand standers-by,
Clapping hands with shout and stare,
What would little Tabby care
For the plaudits of the crowd!
Over happy to be proud,
O'er wealthy in the treasure
Of her own exceeding pleasure.

Their fecund loins are full of magic sparks
And specks of gold, like fine sand,
Add vague stars to their mystical eyes.
                    Charles Baudelaire (1821–1867)

To A Cat
by John Keats (1795–1821)

Cat! who has pass'd thy grand climacteric,
How many mice and rats hast in thy days
Destroy'd?—How many titbits stolen? Gaze
With those bright languid segments green, and prick
Those velvet ears—but prithee do not stick
Thy latent talons in me—and upraise
Thy gentle mew—and tell me all the frays
Of fish and mice, and rats and tender chick...

The Witch
by Heinrich Heine (1797–1856)

"Dear friends next door, forgive the intrusion!
I warn you a witch can cause confusion

By changing through magic her outward form
To that of a beast, to do us harm.

Your cat's my wife! I'm wide awake!
I'm perfectly sure! I can't mistake
Her scent, her sidelong look, her claws
Her noisy purr, her licking of paws."

The man and wife cried out in fear—
"Take back the witch, she shouldn't be here!"
Their watchdog barked and made a row,
But puss, composed, said only "Meow."

Cruel, but composed and bland,
Dumb, inscrutable and grand,
So Tiberius might have sat
Had Tiberius been a cat.

Matthew Arnold (1822–1888)
from "Matthias"

Last Words To A Dumb Friend
by Thomas Hardy (1840–1928)

Pet was never mourned as you,
Purrer of the spotless hue,
Plumy tail, and wistful gaze,
While you humoured our queer ways,
Or outshrilled your morning call
Up the stairs and through the hall—
Foot suspended in its fall—
While, expectant, you would stand
Arched, to meet the stroking hand;

Till your way you chose to wend
Yonder, to your tragic end.

Never another pet for me!
Let your place all vacant be;
Better blankness day by day
Than companion torn away.
Better bid his memory fade,
Better blot each mark he made,
Selfishly escape distress
By contrived forgetfulness,
Then preserve his prints to make
Every morn and eve an ache.

From this chair whereon he sat
Sweep his fur, nor wince thereat;
Rake his little pathways out
Mid the bushes roundabout;
Smooth away his talons' mark
From the claw-worn pine-tree bark,
Where he climbed as dusk embrowned,
Waiting us who loitered round.

. . . .

As a prisoner, flight debarred,
Exercising in a yard,
Still retain I, troubled, shaken,
Mean estate, by him forsaken;
And this home, which scarcely took
Impress from his little look,
By his faring to the Dim,
Grows all eloquent of him.

Housemate, I can think you still
Bounding to the window-sill,

Over which I vaguely see
Your small mound beneath the tree,
Showing in the autumn shade
That you moulder where you played.

A Writer's Cat
by Neville Baybrooke

I remember the day a favorite cat died.
At dawn I carried him into the garden and laid him
   on a bed of mint,
Still breathing.
The eyes I had known for almost thirteen yeas
   followed me about.
When the post arrived, he gave a short purr:

It had been his habit since a kitten.
It was his last link with my world of manuscripts
   and books.
Our parting would be soon.
Later when I wrapped him in an old cardigan
I thought of Anatole France and St. Mael's
   baptism of the penguins
And how St. Catherine had said:
"Give them souls—but tiny ones."

I will settle for that
For my cat.

The Rubaiyat of a Persian Kitten
by Oliver Herford (1863–1935)

> Myself when young, did eagerly frequent,
> The backyard fence and heard great argument,
> About it, and about, yet evermore,
> Came out with fewer fur than in I went.

An Alley Cat's Poem for Mehitabel

> persian pussy from over the sea
> demure and lazy and smug and fat
> none of your ribbons and bells for me
> ours is the zest of the alley cat
> over the roofs from flat to flat
> we prance with capers corybantic
> what though a boot should break a slat
> mehitabel us for the life romantic

> we would rather be rowdy and gaunt and free
> and dine on a diet of roach and rat
> . . . .
> we would rather be rowdy and gaunt and free
> and dine on a diet of roach and rat
> than slaves to a tame society
> ours is the zest of the alley cat
> fish heads freedom a frozen sprat
> dug from the gutter with digits frantic
> is better than bores and a fireside mat
> mehitabel us for the life romantic

> when pendant moon in the leafless tree
> clings and sways like a golden bat

i sing its light and my love for thee
ours is the zest of the alley cat
missiles around us fall rat a tat tat
but our shadows leap in a ribald antic
as over the fences the world cries scat
mehitabel us for the life romantic.

Don Marquis (1878–1937)
from *archy and mehitabel*

Miao
by Dylis Laing (1906–1960)

I put down my book
The Meaning of Zen
And see the cat smiling into her fur
as she delicately combs it with her rough pink tongue.
"Cat, I would lend you this book to study
but it appears that you have already read it."
She looks up and gives me her full gaze.
"Don't be ridiculous," she purrs. "I wrote it."

An excerpt from *War Cat*
by Dorothy Sayers (1893–1957)

I am sorry, my little cat, I am sorry—
if I had it, you should have it;
but there is a war on.
No, there are no table scraps.
Cat with the innocent face,
what can I say?
Everything is very hard on everybody.

If you were a little Greek cat,
or a little Polish cat,
There would be nothing for you at all,
not even cat food;
indeed, you would be lucky
if you were not eaten yourself.
Think if you were a little Russian cat
prowling among the cinders of a deserted city!
Alas! There is no language
in which I can tell you these things.

Wait only a little
and I will go to the butcher
and see if by any chance
he can produce some fragments of the insides of
    something.
Only stop crying
and staring in that unbearable manner—
as soon as I have put on my hat
we will try to do something about it.

My hat is on,
I have put on my shoes,
I have taken my shopping basket—
What are you doing on the table?

The chicken-bowl is licked clean;
there is nothing left in it at all.
Cat,
hell-cat Hitler-cat, human,
all-too-human cat,
cat corrupt, infected,
instinct with original sin,
cat of a fallen and perverse creation,

hypocrite with the innocent and limpid eyes—
is nothing desirable till somebody else desires it?

Is anything and everything attractive
so long as it is got by stealing?
Furtive and squalid cat,
green glance, squinted over a cringing shoulder,
streaking hurriedly out of the back door
in expectation of judgment,
your manners and morals are perfectly abhorrent to
    me,
you dirty little thief and liar.

Nevertheless,
although you have made a fool of me,
yet, bearing in mind your pretty wheedling ways
and having put on my hat to go to the butcher's,
I may as well go.

Four Odes to Honorable Cat
by Paul Gallico (1897–1976)

Rich Cat, Poor Cat

Rich cat, poor cat
Beggar cat, tramp
House cat, alley cat
Store cat, champ.
The rich cat eats from a porcelain dish
Cream and chicken and lobster and fish
Poor cat sups from a dirty old tin
Scraps and bones and bits of skin
If you look at it, it's fair to neither
There ain't no justice in our world either.

The Insult

I have been insulted.
My feelings have been hurt
And I am not coming back into the house.

You laughed at me.
Don't think that I was fooled.
You weren't laughing *with* me
But AT me
When I lost my balance
Washing,
And fell over.
You laughed,
And it wasn't funny.
All my grace, control, and dignity were gone;
You robbed me of my image of myself
And with your braying
All but destroyed my pride.
Don't think I cannot take a joke.
There's nothing lacking with my sense of humor,
I just don't like being made to look ridiculous.
It's no use your standing there calling,
"Kitty, kitty, kitty!"
Or offering me bribes.
Your coarse laughter
Has offended me deeply
And it may take me some time to get over it,
or never.
If and when I come back at all
It will be
In my own sweet time.

The Wizard

Dog, beware!
For I am a great wizard
Who has turned himself into a beast
One hundred cubits tall,

With jaws that gape,
And teeth more fearful than the fangs
Of ancient dragons.
My claws are like the scythes
That armed the wheels of warrior chariots.
My eyes flash fire,
I exhale poisonous smoke,
And could devour you at a bite.
Dog, if you are wise you will agree.
Do not account me
A small and timid creature
Arching its back to try to frighten you.
Just go away and do not compel me
To break my spell
And retire up a tree.

Speech

When I have things to say
I expect you to listen to me.
If you cannot understand what I am saying
That is your fault and your loss,
But at least be quiet when I am speaking
And try to comprehend
You who think yourselves so clever,
Who know languages of the people
Of the living world and the dead,
Why cannot you learn mine
Which is so simple
To express wants so few?
"In"
"Out"
"Hungry"

"Thirsty"

"Give me just a taste of what you are having."

"Something hurts."

"My ball has rolled under the divan; get it out."

"Stop doing whatever it is you are doing and pay more
    attention to me."

"I like you."

"I don't like you."

If you can talk to the Arabs, the Chinese, the Eskimos

And read the hieroglyphics of the past, why cannot you
    understand me?

Try!

from *Honorable Cat*

Cat on the Hearth
by August Derleth (1909–1971)

The languid cat before the fireplace
flexes muscles, laves herself;
she yawns, turns her inscrutable face
to coals' red glow beneath the mantel shelf.
The room revolves about her
where she lies. Outside—cold, moon, snow;
here within this glow her new-washed fur
is summer-sheen. She looks into the dancing flames.
No one knows what she sees there. None bespeaks
    the inner way.
of any cat. Fire beguiles and tames
the huntress of the dark, enchants the playful waif
    of day.

The Kitty-Cat Bird
by Theodore Roethke (1908–1963)

The Kitty-Cat Bird, he sat on a Fence.
Said the Wren, your Song isn't worth 10¢.
You're a Fake, you're a Fraud, you're a Hor-rid
   Pretense!
—Said the Wren to the Kitty-Cat Bird.

You've too many Tunes, and none of them Good:
I wish you would act like bird really should,
Or stay by yourself down deep in the wood,
—Said the Wren to the Kitty-Cat Bird.

You mew like a Cat, you grate like a Jay:
You squeak like Mouse that's lost in the Hay,
I wouldn't be You for even a day.

—Said the Wren to the Kitty-Cat Bird.
The Kitty-Cat Bird, he moped and he cried.
Then a real cat came with a Mouth so Wide,
That the Kitty-Cat Bird just hopped inside;
"At last I'm myself!"—and he up and died

—Did the Kitty—the Kitty-Cat Bird.
You'd better not laugh; and don't say, "Pooh!"
Until you have thought this Sad Tale through:
Be sure that whatever you are is you
—Or you'll end like the Kitty-Cat Bird.

This Muff of Fur
by Mildred R. Howland

The Devil's soul
Is not more black
Than Smudge, my cat
Who has more yen
For mice than men.

Narrowed to slits
His topaz eyes
Fixed on a hole
As there he sits
With fierce control
For hours
And glowers—
Claws curved, intent,
On murder bent.
No angel's smile
Has half the wile
Of his smug purr
In a feigned nap—
This muff of fur
Curled on my lap.

In my castle
He is king
And I his vassal.
Bound to appease,
Beseeching paws
With indrawn claws
Pad my old knees;
He knows how weak
I am—the sneak,

Softer than silk
Close by my side,
Milder than milk

Bless his black hide.

in *Atlantic Monthly*
July 1954

Half Asleep
by Aileen Fisher

To assume a cat's asleep
is a grave mistake.
He can close his eyes and keep
both his ears awake.
from *My Cat Has Eyes of Sapphire Blue*

The Convert
by Paul Jennings

As an immature youth I thought nothing
could be merrier
Than a wire-haired terrier;
I loved dachshunds
That bark with foreign achshunds,
I forgave even Pekinese
For their endless bronchitis, their
yapping, their waddle
suggesting wekinese;
Lugubrious Labradors, sloppy spaniels,
even those crew-cut corgis,
I loved them all, I loved all dorgis.

Then I found that, by any tests,
Dogs are terrible as guests;
We look after somebody's dog, and it
    wanders from room to room,
  all restless and moaning, it doesn't
accept us as master and missus;
A dog says ME ME ME, it's just a
    gauche Narcissus;
But when we leave our cat, she just
    greets her hostess politely,

  then goes to change for dinner in the
  attic.
I've lost my taste for dogs, my taste is
  aristocratic

        *   *   *

I've heard of police dogs, but I bet they
    bite the wrong people;
  I bet they're too stupid to be
  effective.
They only pound the beat; if cats were
  in the police they'd never come
below the rank of detective.

If animals had television,
Dogs would stare at it all day long, but
    cats can entertain
  themselves, singing madrigals with
taste
  and precision,
And one cat alone'll

Give a fair imitation of a modern violin
  concerto, all subtle and atonal—

But when a dog barks (as he does too
   often) he
Sounds like the tearing of giant emery
      paper,
   the world's worst cacophony...

But let me not too harshly end,
I can't quite hate Man's Second Best
   Friend.

in *The Observer*, 1956

Squatter's Rights
by Richard Shaw

Listen, Kitten,
Get this clear;
This is my chair.
I sit here.

Okay, Kitty,
We can share;
When I'm not home,
It's your chair.

Listen Tom Cat,
How about
If I use it
When you're out?

For a Dead Kitten
by Sara Hay

What was warm is strangely cold
When dissolved the little breath?
How could this small body hold
So immense a thing as death?

The Cat
by W. H. Davies (1871–1940)

Within that porch, across the way,
I see two naked eyes this night;
Two eyes that neither shut nor blink,
Search my face with a green light.
But cats to me are strange, so strange—
I cannot sleep if one is near;
And though I'm sure I see those eyes,
I'm not so sure a body's there!

Politeness Counts
by Antoinette Deshoulières (1638–1694)

Always well-behaved am I,
Never scratch and never cry;
Only touch the diner's hand,
So that he can understand
That I want a modest share
Of the good things that are there.
If he pay but scanty heed
To my little stomach's need,

I beg him with a mew polite
To give me just a single bite.
Greedy though that diner be,
He will share his meal with me.

My Old Cat
by Hal Summers

My old cat is dead,
Who would butt me with his head.
He had the sleekest fur.
He had the blackest purr.
Always gentle with us
Was this black puss,
But when I found him today
Stiff and cold where he lay
His look was a lion's
full of rage, defiance:
Oh, he would not pretend
That what came was a friend
But met it in pure hate.
Well died, my old cat.

My Cat and I
by Roger McGough

Girls are simply the prettiest things
My cat and i believe
And we're always saddened
When it's time for them to leave
We watch them titivating
(that often takes a while)

and though they keep us waiting
My cat & i just smile

We like to see them to the door
Say how sad it couldn't last
Then my cat and i go back inside
And talk about the past.

Under-The-Table Manners
Anonymous

It's very hard to be polite
    If you're a cat.
When other folks are up at table
Eating all that they are able,
    You are down upon the mat
    If you're a cat.

You're expected just to sit
    If you're a cat.
Not to let them know you're there
By scratching on the chair,
    Or a light, respected pat
    If you're a cat.

You are not to make a fuss
    If you're a cat.
Tho' there's fish upon the plate
You're expected just to wait,
    Wait politely on the mat
    If you're a cat.

On A Cat Aging
by Alexander Gray

He blinks upon the hearth-rug
And yawns in deep content,
Accepting all the comforts
That Providence has sent.

Louder he purrs, and louder
In one glad hymn of praise,
For all the night's adventures,
For quiet, restful days.

Life will go on for ever,
With all that cat can wish;
Warmth, and the glad procession
Or fish, and milk, and fish.

Only—the thought disturbs him—
He's noticed once or twice,
The times are somehow breeding
A nimbler race of mice.

Our often mysterious Manx
Maintained an especially anx-
Ious Vigil. "I'm be-
Ing tailed," he said. We
Didn't smile. For which he said "Thanx."

Roy Blount, Jr.

To err is human
To purr feline.

Robert Byrne

Billllie The Cat

Billllie the cat,
The wonderful, wonderful cat!
You'll laugh so hard, yer tush will
    ache,
Your heart will go pitter-pat!

Billllie the cat,
The wonderful, marketable cat!
If he can't find a litter box,
He'll head right for your hat!

                    Berke Breathed
                    in the cartoon strip *Bloom County*

From *A Bestiary*
by Kenneth Rexroth (1905–1982)

There are too many poems
About cats. Beware of cat
Lovers, they have a hidden
Frustration somewhere and will
Stick you with it if they can.

Cat Facts

from *The New Columbia Encyclopedia*:

CAT, name applied broadly to the carnivorous mammals constituting the family Felidae and specifically to the domestic cat, *Felis catus*. The great roaring cats, the lion, tiger, jaguar, leopard, and snow leopard are anatomically very similar to one another and constitute the genus *Panthera*.... Of all the carnivores, cats are the most exclusive flesh-eaters and are the most highly adapted for hunting and devouring their prey.... In all but the cheetah, the claws are completely retractile, being withdrawn into protective sheaths when not in use. This mechanism is a distinguishing feature of the cat family.... Most cats have good vision and are able to see well in very dim light; their color vision is weak. Their sense of hearing is excellent and, at least in the small cats, can detect frequencies of up to 40,000 Hz or higher. The sense of smell is not as highly developed as the dog.... Cats are extremely agile; they can run faster than any other mammal for short distances and are remarkable jumpers.... [However,] only the cheetah runs down its prey....

Cats have been domesticated since prehistoric times, perhaps for as long as 5,000 years. (Dogs are believed to have been domesticated for about 50,000 years.) They have been greatly valued as destroyers of vermin, as well as for their ornamental qualities. The ancient Egyptian domestic cat, which spread to Europe in historic times, was used as a retriever in hunting.... It was probably derived from *Felis lybica* or one of the other North African wildcats. The modern domestic cat...is probably descended from this animal, perhaps with an admixture of other wildcat species.... Cats were venerated in the ancient Egyptian and Norse religions; they have also been the object of superstitious fear, especially in the Middle

Ages, when they were tortured and burned as witches. ...[Abyssinians] are thought to be the most unchanged descendants of the ancient Egyptian domestic cat.

In the Beginning

Kitty probably had his ancestral beginnings with the miacis, a bad-mouthed, ill-tempered, weasel-like grouch that roamed the earth about 50,000,000 years ago. It is not known how the unpleasant personality characteristics of the miacis were determined, but possibly archaeologists found fossils of human legs with miacis teethmarks in them.... The cat as we know it today first appeared about 10,000,000 years later. The cats that existed at that time were not typical parlor Persians, but probably more closely resembled the civet, whose anal secretion is one of the most popular fixatives for expensive perfumes....

Curled up on the hearth, he is a member of the family. Once outside the house, however, he reverts to the primitive instincts of his progenitors, stalking and springing, attacking and defending, moaning and howling. But the minute he crosses the threshold of home, he sheds the role of jungle beast. Draping himself in an aura of innocence, he plays the role of pussycat again.

> Helen Powers
> from *The Biggest Little Cat Book in the World*

Cats have succeeded one another through the Tertiary epoch for probably millions of years, and in their capacity as butchering machines have undergone a steady improvement.

> Thomas Henry Huxley (1825–1895)

Ancient Egypt

A rich man's cat was elaborately mummied, wound 'round and 'round with stuff and cunningly plaited with linen ribbons dyed two different colors. His head was encased in a rough kind of papier-mache that was covered with linen and painted, even gilt sometimes, the ears always carefully pricked up. The mummy might be enclosed in a bronze box with a bronze statue of the cat seated on the top. Even a finer burial might await a particularly grand cat. A poor man's cat was rolled up in a simple lump, but the rolling was carefully and respectfully done.

William Martin Conway (1856–1937)

When a cat died, a wise Egyptian tried to be someplace else so that he couldn't be accused of its murder. If a cat died in a private house by a natural death, all the residents shaved their eyebrows.

Herodotus (480–425 B.C.)

By the time of the Pharaohs, cats were pretty much in control of things. Women adopted their graces, as smart women have done ever since. They copied the shape and style of the cats' eyes in their makeup and they copied their mysterious and aloof manner. . . .

Egypt was the great granary of the civilized world. However, the towering warehouses could be seen by every rat and mouse for miles. They took the first road to the granaries they could find. The cat stopped this invasion in its tracks. The priests decided to reward the cat, but they did not want to give him anything tangible. They took the cheap way out. They made the cat a god. In those days this was about the equivalent of being made an assistant vice president of something.

Eric Gurney
How to Live with a Calculating Cat

Ancient Rome

Not a single cat's bone has been found at Pompeii, in spite of the fact that it was regularly visited by Greeks from Egypt. Rome knew so little about the uses of the cat that their rough soldiers and their vain leaders never understood the feelings of Egyptians for their cats. Once when the Nile area was occupied by Caesar and his army, a Roman soldier was mobbed and murdered savagely in a street in Alexandria. The crowd, accusing him of having accidentally killed a cat, threw themselves on him, lynched him, and dragged his corpse the length and breadth of the town. Deaf to the Roman threats of severe reprisals, the Egyptians rose and resistance began. It did not stop until the deaths of Antony and Cleopatra, when Egypt, at last effectively defeated, became a Roman province; and the cat, formerly worshipped, was ostracized.

Fernand Méry
The Life, History and Magic of the Cat

How to See Demons

Find and burn the placenta of the first litter of a black cat, then beat it into a powder and rub it into the eyes.

The Talmud

The Price of a Cat In 948 A. D.

The worth of a kitten from the night it is kittened until it shall open its eyes is a legal penny.

And from that time, until it shall kill mice, two legal pence.

And after it shall kill mice, four legal pence.

If she be bought and be deficient, let one third of her worth be returned.

The worth of a cat that is killed or stolen: its head to be put downwards upon a clean even floor, with its tail lifted upwards, and thus suspended, whilst wheat is poured about it, until the tip of its tail be covered, and that is to be its worth.

The worth of a common cat is four legal pence.

Whoever shall sell a cat is to answer for her not going a caterwauling every moon; and that she devour not her kittens; and that she have ears, eyes, teeth, and nails; and being a good mouser.

The Laws of Hoel the Good, King of Wales

In 1127, nuns were forbidden to wear skins costlier than catskin or lambskin, and in 1205 a proclamation called the Ancrene Wisse forbade them from owning any animal except the cat. ("Ye mine leove sustren ne schulen haben no Beste bute Kat one.")

The catte is a beaste of uncertain hair and colour; for some catte is white, some rede, some black, some spewed and speckled in the fete and in the face and in the eares. And he is in youth swyfte, plyante, and mery, and lepeth and rusheth on all thynge that is before him; and is led by a strawe and playeth therwith. And is a right hevy beast in age, and ful slepy, and lieth slily in wait for myce...and when he taketh a mous he playeth therwith, and eateth him after the play.... And he maketh a ruthefull noyse and gastful when one proffereth to fyght with another.

> Bartholomaeus Anglicus (circa 1250)
> *Of the Nature of Things*

Charles I of England [1600–1649] had a black cat, which he carried with him everywhere he went, claiming that the cat was his luck. When the cat died, the king wailed, "My luck is gone!" He was arrested the next day and later beheaded.

> Leonore Fleischer
> *The Cat's Pajamas*

Those who will keep their cats indoors and from hunting birds abroad must cut off their ears, for they cannot endure to have drops of rain distill into them, and therefore keep themselves in harbor.

> Edward Topsell (1572–1625)
> *Historie of Foure-footed Beasts*

She useth therefore to wash her face with her feet, which she licketh and moiseneth with her tongue; and it is observed by some that if she put her feet beyond the crown of her head in this kind of washing, it is a sign of rain.

> John Swan
> *Speculum Mundi* (1643)

There are some who if a cat accidentally come into the room, though they neither see it nor are told of it, will presently be in a sweat, and ready to die.

> Increase Mather (1639–1723)

Many of the country houses that were built in France between the middle of the sixteenth and seventeenth centuries were equipped with *chatieres*, small openings cut in the door for the accommodation of the cat. By the close of the seventeenth century the *chatieres* were no longer to be found. The cat had trained people to let him in and out.

> Richard C. Smith
> *The Complete Cat Book*

In 1699, at the Swedish town of Mora, 300 children were accused of employing demon cats to steal butter, cheese, and bacon. Fifteen of the children were killed, and every Sunday for a year, 36 were whipped before the church doors.

> *Time*
> December 1981

A Medieval View

A crafty, subtle, watchful Creature, the mortal enemy to the Rat, Mouse, and all sorts of Birds, which it seizes on as its prey. As to its Eyes, Authors say that they shine in the Night, and see better at the full, and more dimly at the change of the Moon.

It is a neat and cleanly Creature, often licking it self, to keep it fair and clean, and washing its Face with its fore-feet. They usually generate in the winter Season, making a great noise.

Its Flesh is not usually eaten, yet in some Countries it is accounted an excellent Dish, but the Brain is said to be poisonous, causing madness, stupidity, and loss of memory, which is cured only by vomiting, and taking

musk in Wine. The Flesh applied easeth the pain of Hae-
morrhoids; and the back, salted, beaten, and applied, draws
Thorns, etc., out of the Flesh, and is said particularly to
help the Gout.

William Salmon
The English Physician

Witch's Incantation for Invisibility

Steal a black cat, buy a new pot, a mirror, a piece of flint,
and agate, charcoal, and tinder; draw water from a foun-
tain at the exact hour of midnight; after that light your
fire, put the cat in the pot, and hold the cover with the
left hand without moving or looking behind you, whatever
noise you may hear, and after it has boiled for twenty-
four hours, always without moving or looking behind you,
put the mess into a new dish, taking the meat and throwing
it over the left shoulder, repeating these words: *Accipe
quod tibi do et nihil amplius.*

To Whip a Cat

The slang phrases "To whip a cat" and "To draw through
the water with a cat" mean to practice a practical joke.
The origin is given in Francis Grose's *Dictionary of the
Vulgar Tongues* (1785) as follows: "A trick often practiced
on ignorant country fellows by laying a wager with them
that they may be pulled through a pond by a cat; the bet
being made, a rope is fastened round the waist of the
person to be catted, and the end thrown across the pond,
to which the cat is also fastened, and three or four sturdy
fellows are appointed to lead and whip the cat; these on

a signal given, seize the end of the rope, and pretending to whip the cat, haul the astonished booby through the water."

The Oxford English Dictionary, which has six columns of fine print on the word cat, cites a 1725 letter to the *London Gazette*: "We hope, sir, that this Nation will be too Wise to be drawn twice through the same Water by the very same Cat."

A statute of 1618 forbids the inhabitants of Ypres the pleasure of hurling a cat from their tower on the second Wednesday of Lent, as had been their honored custom for years.

Agnes Repplier (1855–1950)
The Fireside Sphinx

As late as 1911, a witch-cat was the cause of intense excitement in Pottsville, Pennsylvania, occupying the headlines of *The Public Ledger* for four days.

Ashley Montague and Edward Darling
The Prevalence of Nonsense

In England, the superstitious still hold the cat in high esteem, and oftentimes when observing the weather, attribute much importance to its various movements. Thus, according to some, when they sneeze it is a sign of rain.

T. F. Dyer (1889)

A Literary Survey
by Nelson Antrim Crawford

Extensive writing about cats began with the late seventeenth and early eighteenth centuries in France, when fashionable interest in the animals, stirred by Cardinals Richelieu and Mazarin, was developing. Antoinette Deshoulière's unique tragedy, *La Mort de Cochon* in which cats are the chief characters, was the first work of literature to exploit the new fashion. In 1727, François Augustin Paradis Moncrif published *Les Chats*, the pioneer of a long line of treatises on cats. The book met with instant popularity. Within a year it was reprinted at Rotterdam, and for at least fifteen years edition after edition appeared.

The intelligentsia of the day—clergy, librarians, literateurs, and university professors—were annoyed that a work on cats should sell better than their volumes on theology and their society essays. Pierre Roy, a minor poet, attempted a sarcastic pun or two, whereupon Moncrif, encountering him, knocked him flat on the pavement.

When Moncrif was admitted to the French Academy in 1735, a group of the more sportive members, flushed with brandy, greeted his introduction with meows.

The earliest work of fiction to deal with cats is *The Life and Adventures of a Cat*, a dull and rambling work printed in London for Willoughby Mynors, a clergyman, and presumably written by him, though the author's knowledge of Continental prostitution seems slightly inappropriate to the cloth.

The pioneer of cat anthologies is Domenico Balestrieri's *Labrime in Morto di un Gatto*, published in 1741. It contains a hundred and fifty poems in Hebrew, Greek, French, and Italian by some seventy-five authors.

The most curious work on cats ever written is undoubtedly *An Extraordinary Chace*; or *The Parson and the Cat*, published in 1820 under the pseudonym of William Cowper, Jr., and written, it is supposed, by the Reverend James Everett, a Methodist minister and bookseller who was in a perpetual quarrel with his coreligionists. The story, in verse illustrated with strange wood engravings, tells of a fox-hunting parson on whose head a frightened cat landed, tearing off his wig and exposing him to the derision of the village. The Puritan lesson is drawn that true servants of God will abstain not only from hunting but from organ music and heated churches:

> Thus wide the good man never roves;
> For these ne'er opes his mouth;
> He warms his church with living stones,
> He draws by force of TRUTH.

The earliest American cat book, so far as is known, is Ebenezer Mack's *The Cat Fight*, a gaudy mock-heroic poem published at New York in 1824. It tells the story of the Kilkenny cats in verse reminiscent of Trumbull, Barlow, and the other early nineteenth-century cutups whom pious professors of literature always refer to as the Hartford Wits.

In scientific writings about cats the pioneer was Pierre Samuel du Pont de Nemours, the founder of the Delaware dynasty. He examined in particular their speech, which he found included not only the simple French vowels, but the consonants m, n, g, h, v, and f. Most Europeans had previously thought of a cat as saying only *meow*, that being the popular onomatopoeic representation of their speech. The learned scholar's investigations resulted in the discovery that in Arabic *naoua*, in Chinese *ming*, and in Sanskrit *mandj* and *vid* were used to represent the cat's cry.

from the Foreword to *Cats in Prose and Verse*

The first comic strip cat was Mr. Jack, appearing in Hearst's *New York Journal* in 1899. Drawn by James Swinnerton, this orange and black-striped, urban, woman chasing, bachelor tiger enjoyed a wide readership for over forty years.

Bill Blackbeard and Malcolm Whyte
Great Comic Cats

Fritz the Cat

In 1972, Fritz the Cat, perhaps the best-known underground "comix" character, was brutally murdered by an ostrich named Andrea. It must be admitted, however, that Fritz probably deserved his shocking end; he had gone "establishment" and had become a playboy movie star, hanging around with big-shot Hollywood producers. And, the ostrich contended, he had forced her to degrade herself for him and perform acts that would make even the most lustful bird blush.

Fritz was created in 1959 by Robert Crumb. Fritz was not your average feline. He was a feisty, vulgar, irresponsible, insecure, drug-crazed sex fiend, often involved in illegal and riotous activities.

In 1969, producers Ralph Bakshi and Steve Krantz discussed with Crumb the possibility of making an animated movie of Fritz. Although Crumb says he never agreed to the project, the film was made and released in 1972 without Crumb's name on it. Aware that Fritz was being misused, Crumb executed Fritz with a stroke of his pen and disassociated himself from all other Fritz projects. Fritz's untimely demise was unique in the history of comic cats, but then, so was Fritz.

Bill Blackbeard and Malcolm Whyte
Great Comic Cats

The cat's homing instinct is phenomenal. One family pet, given to friends in California, set out on a 1,400-mile trip back to its original owner in Oklahoma. When the be-draggled cat arrived in Oklahoma 14 months later, it was positively identified by an old hipbone deformity.

The People's Almanac #2

Cool Cats

Cats play an important role in our great cold storage ware-houses. It was originally hoped that a temperature of six degrees above zero would prove too severe for vermin; but rats have that singular adaptability of character with which nature loves to endow the least popular of her creatures. In a few months they were as much at home in the freezing atmosphere as if they had been accustomed to it for generations, and were rearing large families of children, all comfortably clad in coats of double ply. Sur-rounded by wholesome food, they showed the discretion of their ancient race, scoffed at traps, and avoided poi-soned bait.

It was then suggested that cats might learn to bear the rigours of this bitter cold; and a few hardy pioneers were chosen to be forever banished from light and warmth, from sunshine and the joyousness of earth. Four-fifths of them pined and died, martyrs to unpitying commercial-ism; but the great principle which bids the fittest survive, triumphed once more over cruel conditions. Kittens raised in the icy temperature began to look like little polar bears, their fur was so thick and warm. By degrees their ears were hidden under furry caps, their tails grew short and bushy, their delicate whiskers coarse and strong. They preserved their health and developed incredible activity.

At present, cold-storage cats are among the sturdiest of the species; and we are even assured by those that hold them prisoners that they enjoy their dark captivity and would be wretched if returned to normal conditions.

Agnes Repplier (1855–1950)
The Fireside Sphinx

If the cat continues to show distress in its new home, try smearing butter on its paws and legs. The cat will be so distracted by its need to lick them clean that it will forget all about its unhappiness over the move....

The cat is the only animal—other than the camel and the giraffe—to walk by moving its front and hind legs on one side, then the other.

William H. A. Carr
The Basic Book of the Cat

The cat is able, when she falls, to turn in the air and land squarely on her feet. Some cats were held by an investigator in a horizontal position with their backs to the floor. The cats invariably made the rotation as soon as support was removed. All were able to land perfectly even when the distance of the fall was only one foot. Some were able to turn in six inches.

Georgia Strickland Gates
The Modern Cat: Her Mind and Manners

Left-Handed Cats

Dr. J. Michael Warren, director of the Animal Behavior Laboratory at Penn State, spent more than a year testing cats and found them almost evenly divided in preference for the right forepaw and the left forepaw in delicate food-snatching assignments. Indeed, the proportions of right to left was nine to eight.

Ashley Montague and Edward Darling
The Prevalence of Nonsense

A feline trauma known as High-Rise Syndrome is being seen by veterinarians with increasing frequency, warns the American Society for Prevention of Cruelty to Animals. Cats that live in apartment buildings and are not allowed outside often sit on window sills. If the window is open, a cat may lose his footing and fall, or he may lose his head and leap at a bird.

Cats, unlike dogs and humans, have an exceptionally efficient righting mechanism, and usually fall with the head down, like a diver. The most common injuries, therefore, are broken jaws, broken front legs, and ruptured lungs. The fall can be fatal, but cats have fallen from amazing heights and survived. The records are: 18 stories onto a hard surface, 20 stories onto shrubbery, and 28 stories onto an awning.

If a cat does not die from a fall and is treated within 20 minutes, he will probably survive.

Cat Fancy magazine
March 1983

New! Cat I.Q. Test!
Just how smart is your cat?

Smarter than a lot of people imagine! So smart that with the help of the "Kitty Whiz Transfer System"® almost any cat can learn to use the bathroom toilet in just a few minutes. With a toilet trained cat there is no mess, odor, expense or bother. And if you are queasy about a cat

sitting on your toilet seat, just keep the seat up. Your cat will be just as comfortable sitting on the porcelain rim. Does not interfere with normal use of toilet. After a few days "Kitty Whiz"® is removed and cat will continue to use the toilet automatically! It's just that simple! Kick the kitty litter blues habit! Order your "Kitty Whiz Transfer System"® today! ($14.95 ppd. without Plush Flush®; $19.95 ppd. with Plush Flush®)

> from an advertisement in *Cats* magazine
> February 1983

If you stroke your black cat in a dark room when the temperature is around zero and the air is dry, you will see sparks. Put this on your list of entertaining things to do during the winter blackout....

The cat's male sex organs will look like two dots or a colon (:) beneath its tail, while the female will resemble an inverted exclamation point (¡). If your new cat is a (¡) it will have kittens. If it is a (:) it will spray on your drapes.

> Helen Powers
> *The Biggest Little Cat Book in the World*

Pets Bite Pocketbooks

Your local animal shelter might be urging you to adopt a dog or cat, but before you do, contemplate the financial obligation you may be undertaking. The cost of getting a pet from a private home, shelter, or humane society may run only $5 to $50, says the Bide-A-Wee Home Association—vs. $100 to $300 if you go to a pet shop or $350 to $400 from a breeder. That, however, is just the beginning.

Feeding a 10-lb. dog costs, on average, $105 a year, while one that weighs 40 lb. will eat $316 worth of food and an 80-lb. canine will devour $527 worth. You can also expect to pay about $180 in veterinary bills during the first year of a dog's life, about $136 for a cat's. During the next eight years, medical bills typically will total only $115 to $145 for the entire period. But in the pet's final year, medical and burial charges will cost you $200 to $385.

Adding in costs for boarding, toys, grooming, licenses, and, in some cases, fencing the yard, veterinarian Steven B. Holzman concludes that an average small dog costs its owner $3,500 over a 10-year life span and a large one, $8,350. A cat costs $4,000.

Foreknowledge of the costs, hopes New York City—based Bide-A-Wee, may dissuade some people from taking on a pet only to abandon it later when they become disenchanted. And, an official points out, even the most expensive dog provides love and companionship for just 10 cents an hour over its lifetime.

Business Week
October 4, 1982

To Each His Own

Unlike puppies, each kitten has its own teat on the mother's belly and does not change from one to another.

> Leon F. Whitney
> *Training You to Train Your Cat*

World Record Cats (Allegedly)

Two cats from Devonshire, England, are thought to be the oldest that ever lived. "Puss" died in 1939 at the age of 36 and "Ma" died in 1957 at the age of 34.

The fattest cat might have been "Spice," of Ridgefield, Connecticut, which scaled 43 pounds in 1974 and died in 1977.

"Bluebell," of Wellington, South Africa, gave birth to 14 live kittens in December of 1974.

"Dusty," of Bonham, Texas, produced her 420th kitten on June 12, 1952.

Between 1927 and 1933, a female tabby named "Minnie" killed 12,480 rats at White City Stadium, London. A tabby named "Mickey" killed 22,000 mice between 1945 and 1968 in Lancashire, England.

Source: *The Guinness Book of World Records*

Purring is not a "voice" coming from the larynx but is the vibration of the blood in a large vein in the chest cavity. Where the vein passes through the diaphragm, contraction of muscles "nips" the blood flow and sets up oscillations, the sounds of which are magnified by the air-filled bronchial tubes and windpipe.

David Taylor
The Cat: An Owner's Maintenance Manual

Miscellany II

Adlai's Choice

I cannot agree that it should be the declared public policy of Illinois that a cat visiting a neighbor's yard or crossing the highway is a public nuisance. It is in the nature of cats to do a certain amount of unescorted roaming.... To escort a cat about on a leash is against the nature of the cat.... Moreover, cats perform useful service, particularly in rural areas.... The problem of cat versus bird is as old as time. If we attempt to resolve it by legislation, who knows but what we may be called upon to take sides as well in the age-old problems of dog versus cat, bird versus bird, or even bird versus worm. In my opinion, the State of Illinois and its local governing bodies have enough to do without trying to control feline delinquency.

> Adlai Stevenson (1900–1965)
> Governor of Illinois
> vetoing a cat leash law in 1949

Most cats have trained their owners. When the cat meows before the refrigerator, the owner obediently opens the door and feeds the cat. When it meows at the back door, the owner is trained to let the cat out.

> Leon F. Whitney
> *Training You to Train Your Cat*

Drunks

There are occasional references in literature to cats with a taste for liquor. According to Carl Van Vechten, W. Lauder Lindsay (1880) mentions a cat who was fond of port. Jerome K. Jerome (1893) writes of another who drank from a leaking beer tap until she was intoxicated.

Van Vechten also quotes a note (1879) from Miss Savage to Samuel Butler in which she reports her cat's liking for mulled port and rum punch. More recently, Doreen Tovey (1970) speaks of "two sleek young Seal Points from Chelsea who drank sherry." Dell Shannon's popular mystery stories featuring Lieutenant Luis Mendoza of the Los Angeles Police Department include a cat named El Señor who is addicted to rye whiskey.

To find out whether these anecdotal and fictional tipplers have present-day company, a telephone poll of fourteen Chicago-area veterinarians was undertaken. None of the fourteen had ever had a feline patient who needed drying out, and ten of them had never heard of cats with a taste for alcoholic beverages. Four knew, or knew of, such cats. One took beer by licking it from its owner's finger, another drank it from a saucer, and a third liked martinis. All the polled veterinarians, however, have had to minister to tipsy dogs.

Muriel Beadle
The Cat

Neurotic cats will often seek alcoholic drinks which they have learned will ameliorate their neuroses.

Leon F. Whitney
Training You to Train Your Cat

We should doff our hats to Jack, a black tom living in Brooklyn, who in 1937 at the age of three gave up drinking water for milk laced with Pernod. As he grew older he demanded stiffer and stiffer saucers of "milk" until it was a question of lacing the Pernod lightly with milk. Jack gave up the ghost in the bar where he lived when he was eight years old. At the post mortem his liver was found to be in a sad state. Jack might have been interested to know that cats given steady alcoholic diets appear to be more resistant to atomic radiation than their teetotal brethren.

David Taylor
The Cat: An Owner's Maintenance Manual

My grandmother's cat, after living a blameless life for upwards of eleven years, took to drink in her old age and was run over while in a state of intoxication (oh, the justice of it!) by a brewer's dray. I have read in temperance tracts that no dumb animal will touch a drop of alcoholic liquor. My advice is, if you wish to keep them respectable, don't give them a chance to get at it.

A leaky beer-tap was the cause of her downfall. A saucer used to be placed underneath to catch the drippings. One day the cat, coming in thirsty and finding nothing else to drink, lapped up a little, liked it, and lapped a little more, went away for half an hour, and came back and finished the saucerful—then sat down beside it and waited for it to fill up again.

From that day till the hour she died, I don't think that cat was ever once sober. Her days she passed in a drunken stupor before the kitchen fire. Her nights she spent in the beer cellar.

My grandmother, shocked and grieved beyond expression, gave up her beer barrel and adopted bottles. The cat, thus condemned to enforced abstinence, meandered about the house for a day and a half in a disconsolate, quarrelsome mood. Then she disappeared, returning at eleven o'clock as tight as a drum.

Where she went, and how she managed to procure the drink, we never discovered; but the same program was repeated every day. Some time during the morning she would contrive to elude our vigilance and escape; and late every evening she would come reeling home across the fields in a condition that I will not sully my pen by attempting to describe.

It was on Saturday night that she met the sad end to which I have before alluded. She must have been very drunk, for the man told us that, because of the darkness and because his horses were tired, he was proceeding at little more than a snail's pace.

I think my grandmother was relieved. She had been very fond of the cat at one time, but its recent conduct had alienated her affection. We children buried it in the garden under the mulberry tree, but the old lady insisted that there should be no tombstone, not even a raised mound. So it lies there, unhonored, in a drunkard's grave.

Jerome K. Jerome (1859–1927)

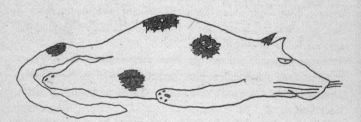

Playing with a Cat

The ability to play successfully with a cat is an exercise in imagination, for it demands entering the world of a very different creature. Games with cats are unlike any others. Any breach of the rules on the part of the human player is likely to bring the game to an abrupt end. The cat, of course, never breaks a rule. If it does not follow precedent, that simply means that it has created a new rule and it is up to you to learn it quickly if you want the game to continue.

Sidney Denham
Our City

I've got to get a pair of cat handcuffs and I've got to get them right away. The little ones that go around the front paws. I found out that my cat was embezzling from me. You know a cat for ten years and then it pulls something like that. I found out that while I was away he would go out to the mailbox, pick up the checks, and go down to the bank and cash them. Disguised as me. He had the kiddie arrow through the head and the kiddie bunny ears. I wouldn't have caught him, but I went outside to his house where he sleeps and I found $3,000 worth of cat toys! You can't return them because they have spit all over them. So I am stuck with $3,000 worth of cat toys. Sure, they're fun...there's a little rubber mouse with a bell inside; boy, I hate it when it goes under the sofa.

Steve Martin

If human, cats might play solitaire, but they would never sit around with the gang and a few six packs watching Monday Night Football.

> *Time*
> December 7, 1981

I'm always outraged and saddened when I hear from a young couple who have been warned that their cats will suffocate a new baby. How on earth do these wild tales start? I don't know of any documented case of a cat harming a baby. The belief that a cat will suffocate or suck the breath out of a baby seems to be about as common today as it was a hundred years ago and just as ridiculous.

> Susie Page
> *Cats* magazine
> February 1983

Cats, like cars, tend to get stolen, scratched, and weather-worn if parked outside night after night.

> David Taylor
> *The Cat: An Owner's Maintenance Manual*

A Cat Nightmare
by Lynette Combs

'Twas the night before Christmas
And all through the house
Not a creature was stirring
Not even a mouse.

I don't know if dog people know other dog people, or if parakeet people know other parakeet people. But cat people always seem to know other cat people. I think we seek each other out, and though we never really say it to each other, we consider ourselves superior to people who don't have or appreciate cats. I think what makes us feel superior is not that we have a cat in our homes, but that a cat has found us acceptable to live with. . . .

When a cat is in the mood, it may give a lick or two with its rough tongue or it may leap into a lap and settle down. But none of these small miracles occurs because some human being has snapped his or her fingers or whistled. To a cat, human beings are an inferior, servile race, always to be kept in their places, with occasional rewards if they perform well. To love a cat is uphill work, and therefore very rewarding.

Haskel Frankel
in the Foreword to Dr. Louis J. Camuti's
All My Patients Are Under the Bed

A Cat's Thought

Picking a human being is like chasing a squirrel in a drain pipe. Sometimes you can't back out even if you want to.

Raymond D. Smith
Cats magazine
February 1982

...a cat at rest with me in the same room is what I like best. The curl-up in a perfect circle or sometimes with one paw over its eyes as though to shut out the light; the hunker with all four feet tidily tucked under, or the sit-up with its tail neatly tucked around its bottom. The poses I know are sheer vanity, for cats are indeed vain and like to be admired. But they will choose backgrounds and put themselves into positions which they know are admirable. They will drape their bodies to the shape of a piece of furniture. They will hang a paw in what seems to be a wholly casual manner, but you know and they know damn well that it is studied. But it is never wrong. Merely by the turn of their heads upon their necks, a half an inch or so, they can change the picture and give expression to

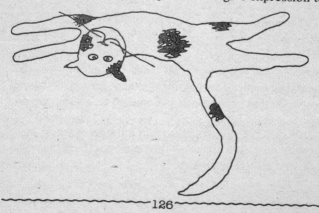

some inner feeling and, by doing so, set up a glow of appreciation in the watcher.

...as for words, they define less than House Cat illustrates them: aesthetic, sublime, tragic, comic, symmetry, supremacy, dignity, charm and grace; in short, the beautiful.

Paul Gallico (1897–1976)
Honorable Cat

Still More Cat People

BARBARA LEDERBERG
She got the name of Frizbee because when she was young she would be running through a room and suddenly jump up and off the wall—six feet into the air, hit the wall and change direction at the same time and be off somewhere else. She does come when you call, but only after you've given up.

SEYMOUR AND PAULA CHWAST
Getting a cat is a greater commitment than getting married.

DAN GREENBURG
Cats are dangerous companions for writers because cat watching is a near-perfect method of writing avoidance. Cats are not people. It's important to stress that because excessive cat watching often leads to the delusion that cats ARE people. There is, incidentally, no way of talking about cats that enables one to come off as a sane person.

TERRY FUGATE-WILCOX AND VALERIE SHAKESPEARE
It's very easy to train cats—just pick anything they like to do and tell them to do it.

JANE PAULEY
You can't look at a sleeping cat and feel tense.

as given in Bill Hayward's
Cat People

The cat is the only animal without visible means of support who still manages to find a living in the city.

Carl Van Vechten (1880–1964)

Cats are rather delicate creatures and they are subject to a good many ailments, but I never heard of one who suffered from insomnia.... Cats seem to go on the principle that it never does any harm to ask for what you want.

Joseph Wood Krutch (1893–1970)

Cats know how to obtain food without labor, shelter without confinement, and love without penalties.

Walter Lionel George (1882–1926)

Cats always know whether people like or dislike them. They do not always care enough to do anything about it.

Winifred Carriere
Cats 24 Hours a Day

The way to keep a cat is to try to chase it away.

E. W. Howe (1853–1937)

Most cats, when they are Out want to be In, and vice versa, and often simultaneously.

Dr. Louis J. Camuti

A kitten is chiefly remarkable for rushing about like mad at nothing whatever, and generally stopping before it gets there.

Agnes Repplier (1855–1950)

Every contented cat is an "it."

Helen Powers on the virtue of neutering

The ideal of calm exists in a sitting cat.

Jules Renard (1864–1910)

Q. What about the way cats claw the upholstery?
A. Learn to like fringe.

Missy Dizick

"Edgar, please run down to the shopping center right away and get some milk and cat food. Don't get canned tuna, or chicken, or liver, or any of those awful combinations. Shop around and get a surprise. The pussies like surprises."

George Booth cartoon caption

B. Kliban's cats are an odd assortment of striped and sometimes sneakered felines who were an instant hit when they were introduced to the public in 1975. Generally defined as "One hell of a nice animal, frequently mistaken for a meatloaf," Kliban's cats are now the center of a $50 million spin-off empire. Kliban's humor is razor edged, and his drawings sometimes border on the grotesque. "Man lying to a cat," for example, is no ordinary title for a kitty cartoon. Nor is the following an ordinary theme song: "Love to eat them mousies/Mousies what I love to eat/ Bite they little heads off/Nibble on they tiny feet."

The artist is uncomfortable with his success and with the blizzard of fan mail it has produced. Kliban's recent collections have been conspicuously empty of cats. "Cats are wonderful," Kliban once said. "It's drawings of cats I get tired of."

J. C. Suares
Great Cats

I get very sentimental about pets. That's why I don't want another one. When they died, it nearly did me in.

B. Kliban

Interview in *Rolling Stone*

At times I feel a bit silly drawing funny pictures of kitty cats for a living. Perhaps I shouldn't feel that way; after all, there are even sillier people paying me to do it.

Quite frankly, I treat Garfield as a human in a cat suit. Cats are perfect for comics. Several of Garfield's personal traits, such as overeating, over-sleeping, and not exercising are endearing in cats and disgusting in humans.

Jim Davis

in the Foreword to *Great Comic Cats*

Cartoonist Jim Davis, thirty-seven, has seen his feline creation Garfield [named after his grandfather] grow in four and a half years into an international marketing sensation. This fat, lazy cat, with few social graces, appears daily in thirteen hundred newspapers.

Davis, who grew up on a farm and is a dropout from Ball State University in Muncie, Indiana [where he lives], does not own a cat. His wife is allergic to them.

"Garfield is an international character. I don't use rhyming gags, plays on words, or colloquialisms in an effort to make Garfield apply to virtually any society where he may appear. In an effort to keep the gags broad, the humor general and applicable to everyone, I deal mainly with eating and sleeping. By virtue of being a cat, Garfield's not black, white, male or female, young or old or a particular nationality.

"A typical Sunday strip in color takes me about four to six hours, the daily from an hour to an hour and a half. The other 60 hours a week is just messing around, licensing, doing promotions, things like that. Just signing fan mail takes many hours a week. One of the advantages of being self-employed is you get to work many more hours than a normal employed person."

Jim Davis
Interviewed in *The Washington Post*

Garfield, in short, is one fat cat.

What brought on all this catomania is a question that should give social scientists paws for reflection; perhaps Darwin was wrong, and maybe all of humankind stemmed from cats instead of apes. Whatever its origins, the nation's feline fetish first became apparent in 1973, when George Gately introduced *Heathcliff*, Garfield's cartoon cousin. Two years later cartoonist Bernard Kliban's whimsical album *Cats* hit the best-seller list. Since then there have been 250 cat books. "Cats rule the world," Davis says. "I don't think it's just a fad. When you're through with your cat, you can't throw it in the trash."

People
November 1, 1982

With five titles on *The New York Times* trade paperback best-seller list, Jim Davis's fractious feline broke his own record (he'd captured four places in March 1982) and further outstripped the competition (Leo Buscaglia once had three, and a handful of other writers, including John Irving this week, have had two).

Explanations they're mulling over at Ballantine: Garfield attracts two large groups of paperback buyers, cat lovers and cat haters; humor books do well in hard times; the syndicated Garfield strip continuously spurs interest in the books.

The New York Times Book Review
October 17, 1982

With the debut of "Garfield Treasury" on the trade paperback list, devotees will note that there are now seven Garfield books there, altogether accounting for 37% of the list's sales.

The New York Times Book Review
November 1, 1982

Garfield Speaks

- Show me a good mouser and I'll show you a cat with bad breath.
- I'm a lasagna with fur and fangs.
- Cat food? The bouquet leaves something to be desired.
- Lasagna is nature's most perfect food.
- When the lasagna content in my blood gets low, I get mean.
- Television commercials are too short for a trip to the sandbox.
- Dogs are rusting our nation's fireplugs.
- What do you expect of me anyway? I'm only human.
- Cute rots the intellect.
- Life's like a hot bath; feels good while you're in it but the longer you stay the more wrinkled you get.
- There must be more to a cat's life, but I hope not.
- I'm fat and lazy and proud of it.
- I never met a lasagna I didn't like.
- They say a cat always lands on its feet, but they don't mention the pain.

Letters, Essays, &
Fiction

From Mark Twain

October 2, 1908
Redding, Connecticut

Dear Mrs. Patterson:
If I can find a photograph of my "Tammany" and her
kittens, I will enclose it in this. One of them likes to be
crammed into a corner pocket of the billiard table—which
he fits as snugly as does a finger in a glove, and then he
watches the game (and obstructs it) by the hour, and spoils
many a shot by putting out his paw and changing the
direction of a passing ball. Whenever a ball is in his arms,
or so close to him that it cannot be played upon without
risk of hurting him, the player is privileged to remove it
to any of the 3 spots that chances to be open.

Sincerely yours,
S. I. Clemens

Two from Thomas Henry Huxley

April 12, 1893
Hodelsea, Eastbourne

(to J. C. Kitton)

A long series of cats has reigned over my household for

the last forty years, but I am sorry that I have no pictorial or other record of their physical and moral excellences.

The present occupant of the throne is a large, young, gray tabby, Oliver by name. Not that he is in any sense a protector, for I doubt whether he has the heart to kill a mouse. However, I saw him catch and eat the first butterfly of the season, and trust that this germ of courage, thus manifested, may develop with age into efficient mousing.

As to sagacity, I should say that his judgement respecting the warmest place and the softest cushion in a room is infallible; his punctuality at meal times is admirable; and his pertinacity in jumping on people's shoulders, till they give him some of the best of what is going on, indicates great firmness.

January 8, 1893
Hodelsea, Eastbourne

(to his youngest daughter)

I wish you would write seriously to M. She is not behaving well to Oliver. I have seen handsomer kittens, but few more lively and energetically destructive. Just now he scratched away at something that M says cost 13s. 6d. a yard and reduced it more or less to combings.

M therefore excluded him from the dining room, and all those opportunities of higher education which he would naturally have in my house.

I have argued that it is as immoral to place 13s. 6d. a yardnesses within reach of kittens as to hang bracelets and diamond rings in the front garden. But in vain. Oliver is banished—and the protector (not Oliver) is sat upon. In truth and justice, aid your Pa.

From Robert Southey

June 18, 1824
Keswick, England

(to his daughter)

Some weeks ago Hurlyburlybuss was manifestly emaciated and enfeebled by ill health, and Rumpelstilzchen with great mangnanimity made overtures of peace. The whole progress of the treaty was seen from the parlour window. The caution with which Rumpel made his advances, the sullen dignity with which they were received, their mutual uneasiness when Rumpel, after a slow and wary approach, seated himself whisker to whisker with his rival, the mutual fear which restrained not only teeth and claws, but even all tones of defiance, the mutual agitation of their tails which, though they did not expand with anger, could not be kept still for suspense, and lastly the manner in which Hurly retreated, like Ajax still keeping his face towards his old antagonist, were worthy to have been represented by that painter who was called the Rafaelle of Cats. The overture I fear was not accepted as generously as it was made; for no sooner had Hurlyburlybuss recovered strength than hostilities were recommenced with greater violence than ever. Rumpel, who had not abused his superiority while he possessed it, had acquired meantime a confidence which made him keep the field. Dreadful were the combats which ensued, as their ears, faces and legs witness. Rumpel had a wound which went through one of his feet. The result had been so far in his favour that he no longer seeks to avoid his enemy, and we are often compelled to interfere to separate them. Oh it is awful to hear the dreadful note of preparation with which they prelude their encounters! The long low growl slowly rises and swells till it becomes a high sharp yowl, and then it is snapt short by a sound which seems as if they were spitting fire and venom at each other. I could half persuade myself that the word felonious is derived from the feline temper and making them understand how goodly a thing it is for cats to dwell together in peace, and what fools they are to quarrel and tear each, are in vain. The proceedings of the Society for the Abolition of War are not more utterly ineffectual and hopeless.

All we can do is to act more impartially than the Gods did between Achilles and Hector and continue to treat them both with equal regard.

From Evelyn Underhill
(1875–1941)

Of course I agree that animals too are involved in the Fall and await redemption and transfiguration. (Do you remember Luther looking up from Romans viii. 21 and say-

ing to his dog, "Thou too shalt have a little golden tail"?)
And man is no doubt offered the chance of being the
mediator of that redemption. But not by taming, surely.
Rather by loving and reverencing the creatures enough
to leave them free. When my cat goes off on her own
occasions I'm sure she goes with God—but I do not feel
so sure of her theological position when she is sitting on
the best chair before the drawing-room fire.

From Sylvia Townsend Warner
(1893–1978)

I wish you could see the two cats, drowsing side by side
in a Victorian nursing chair, their paws, their ears, their
tails complementally adjusted, their blue eyes blinking
open on a single thought of when I shall remember it's
their suppertime. They might have been composed by
Bach for two flutes.

From the Diary of a Young Girl
by Anne Frank (1929–1944)

We were sitting in the attic doing some French yesterday
afternoon when I suddenly heard water pattering down
behind me. I asked Peter what it could be, but he didn't
even reply, simply tore up to the loft, where the source
of the disaster was, and pushed Mouschi [the cat], who,
because of the wet earth box had sat down beside it,
harshly back to the right place. A great din and disturb-
ance followed, and Mouschi, who had finished by that
time, dashed downstairs.

Mouschi, seeking the convenience of something similar
to his box, had chosen some wood shavings. The pool
had trickled down from the loft into the attic immediately
and, unfortunately, landed just beside and in the barrel

of potatoes. The ceiling was dripping, and as the attic floor is not free from holes, either, several yellow drips came through the ceiling into the dining room between a pile of stockings and some books, which were lying on the table. I was doubled up with laughter; it really was a scream. There was Mouschi crouching under a chair, Peter with water, bleaching powder, and floor cloth, and Van Daan trying to soothe everyone. The calamity was soon over, but it's a well-known fact that cats' puddles positively stink. The potatoes proved this only too clearly and also the wood shavings that Daddy had collected in a bucket to be burned. Poor Mouschi! How were you to know that peat is unobtainable?

Cats I Have Known and Loathed
By Gilbert Millstein

For reasons I do not know and have small intention of finding out, the world is afflicted (there is no other word for it) by a tyranny (there is no other word for *that*, either) of cats; cats themselves; novels and poems about and yes, ostensibly *by* cats; things for cats to eat, wear, sit on, sleep on, meditate over and scratch; cat paintings, drawings and cartoons in awful proliferation. On television there is a cat food commercial featuring a fat, complacent animal speaking in Larchmont Lockjaw, a kind of English in which the lips are barely parted and the teeth stay firmly clenched; I have always disliked Larchmont Lockjaw, even in Katharine Hepburn. And, I often wonder what got into cat people like Eliot, Baudelaire and Kipling, among others. I am, *malheureusement*, acquainted with a highly competent cat doctor who addresses bills to the *cat*, care of the owner, and makes believe that the bills come from one of *his* cats. Is it cynical of me to note the checks are invariably made out to the doctor?

Mine is the exhilarating ignorance and unreasoning bad temper of the know-nothing, as far as cats are concerned, and the years have done much to reinforce this. I know of a lady psychologist who loves cats. Inordinately. She owns, oh, hundreds of them and keeps them on two floors of a small building over a defunct nightclub. I will not say where. And she cannot bear to give any of them up. Indeed, when one of them dies, she wraps it in plastic, attaches a name tag, and puts it in a deep freeze she keeps on the third floor. She has lived in the building a long time; I don't know how big the freezer is; and I plan not to go to her for therapy.

Once upon a time, I acquired a lady who owned a cat, male. He didn't like me from the outset. In all fairness, he must have smelled the distaste in me, but how is one to feel about arrogance of the kind displayed by that enormous thing? He used to sit on the arm of a chair, pettishly ripping it open; or, occasionally, knock something down (usually something which, once broken, could not be put together again), all the while hissing in contempt. He made me feel more inferior than I ordinarily do and he got me to drinking more than I ordinarily do and to chasing him under couches from which he could not pulled out. I didn't need that much exercise.

The end came one hot summer night, the end for the cat. I am accustomed to sleeping on my back. At about 4 o'clock in the morning, I was awakened. Something was treading—leisurely, thoughtfully and determinedly—on a part of me never before trod upon. A street lamp shone into the room and was reflected by two great blue disembodied coals burning at me. It was the cat; his claws were unsheathed, and I arose with strangled cries of pain. I know that the *castrato* once had his place in opera, but that was centuries ago. I'm not much of a singer, anyway, and I got away with a few claw rakes. The cat was boarded out the next morning; the lady, too, left eventually, and I continued on my way sullen but intact.

That was a long time ago. The other day, I fell into conversation about cats with a lady who owns six of them. I say fell because she had given me a drink and I had stumbled over something called a scratching post while changing chairs, and barked my right shin. Besides, all six of her cats were posed in alarming attitudes all around the living room, staring at me. Balefully. All cats stare balefully and I have never become accustomed to it. Maddened by drink and annoyed by the pain in my shin, I put a deliberately provocative question to her. "Why," I asked, "do you like cats?" She answered me, I am sorry to say. She said, "Because I am a cat." That got me nervous and I left. We all have our dirty little secrets. That was hers and I have mine.

Mine is that I, too, have a cat. *Mea maxima culpa.* Some men are born to cats, others have cats thrust upon them. This one is alley, female, cross-grained. She hates my son, but that may be only because the blameless child once shot rubber darts at her and got one of his little playmates to do the same thing, and both of them laughing innocently all the while. But that happened a long time ago and I can't see why a cat should carry a grudge so long. We have long since forgiven the Japanese and the Germans, *nicht wahr?*

I subscribe to the conspiracy theory of history. That cat was foisted upon me eight years ago by my wife and her daughter (their very lives are a round of conspiracies—successful ones—to best me) on the implausible theory that they would mind it and it would stay out of my way. They came home casually with this mewling kitten and announced that they had just somehow . . . they weren't sure . . . they . . . and so on. They said they got it free. There is no such thing as a free cat. Veterinarians. Shots. Food. Carrying case. The list is unending.

It scratches maddeningly on the bedroom door every morning at 5:45 and demands in a loud voice to be fed—which it is, by me, of course. It lies across my belly while I am trying to read and if I pet it the wrong way it sometimes snarls, sometimes scratches, sometimes does both and then runs off to eat some more and sulk. And yet, for some reason, it has fixed most of its dubious attentions on me. It barely tolerates my wife and daughter and it loathes friend and stranger alike. It is a curmudgeon and it inspires me to a bromide: I can only suspect that it takes one to know one.

I also suspect something else: that I love the damned cat. For one thing, it shares almost every one of my prejudices. For another, it rubs me the right way. And for a third, I reserve the right, like the cat, to be completely illogical.

> from *The New York Times Magazine*
> March 13, 1977

Seeing-Eye Cats
by Brian McConnachie

In 1968 the Department of the Army began experimenting with the use of "night eyes," or seeing-eye cats. The Army had, for a long time, been quietly impressed with the night vision of cats. The mission of the project was to employ this special ability; harnessed cats were to lead foot-soldiers through the thick jungle during the dead of night.

... After a month of night maneuvering with the seeing-eye cats, a report was filed with the section on Unconventional Warfare, which, in part, stated:

"...A squad, upon being ordered to move out, was led off in all different directions by the cats.

"...On many occasions the animals led the troops racing through thick brush in pursuit of field mice and birds.

"...Troops had to force the cats to follow the direction of the patrol; the practice often led to the animals stalking and attacking the dangling pack straps of the American soldier marching directly in front of the animal.

"...If the weather was inclement or even threatening inclemency, the cats were never anywhere to be found.

"...Often when the troops were forced to take cover, the animals took the opportunity to sharpen their claws on the boots of the troops, regardless of the seriousness of the situation."...

The project was suspended.

from *Cat Catalog*

Mad Anthony
by Dereck Williamson

The tall weeds of September remind me of Mad Anthony, who people said was a little crazy. They were wrong. Mad Anthony was my cat, and I knew he was a lot crazy.

Mad Anthony liked high grass and watering cans. And he liked playing dog.

On a day like this, I would whistle up Mad Anthony, and he would climb out of his watering can where he sat and thought about being a dog. He would trot up to me and wag his tail. Then we'd go for a walk, just a boy and his furry little dog along a country road.

We would stop to look at butterflies and bugs and birds. Mad Anthony would heel. Sometimes he would point. But once in a while he'd get excited, forget he was playing dog, and revert to his natural role of insane cat. He would spring.

Mad Anthony was the only cat I knew who sprang straight up. He never leaped toward a butterfly, bug, or bird. He rose vertically, at least two feet, often three. Whether there was wildlife nearby or not. There was no warning, and the effect was startling. When Mad Anthony sprang, it was as if he'd been standing on a land mine. All of a sudden—*boingg!*

People were amazed. They asked me why my cat leaped up that way for no reason. I told them he was a very special cat. Privately, I thought it was because he was nuts. But I didn't say that because I didn't want to hurt his feelings.

We were good friends. We played a game in the tall grass. Mad Anthony scurried into the field and hid. But not too well. He twitched his tail, so I could see weeds moving. Then I ran into the field, straight at him. *Boingg!*—

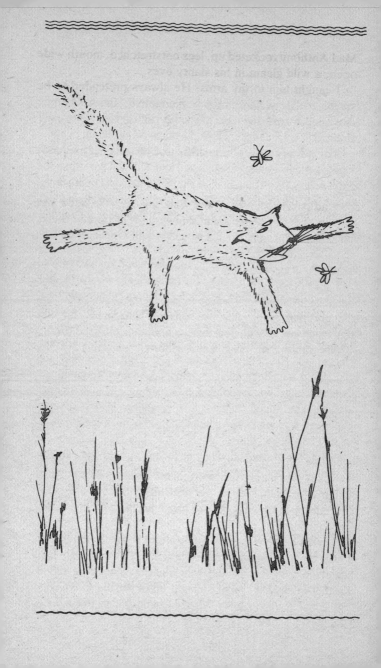

Mad Anthony rocketed up, legs outstretched, mouth wide open, a wild gleam in his slanty eyes.

I caught him in my arms. He always pretended to be surprised. He yelled "Yeow!" a couple of times. Then he struggled to get down so he could run off and do it over again.

The game could take up most of the day. My mother would ask me where I'd been, and I'd say catching the cat.

Mad Anthony lived in the watering can. We left it out all winter for him. He spent an awful lot of time in there. I wondered what he found to do. My parents said he was probably redecorating.

Early in the morning I would tiptoe out of the house and try to sneak up on Mad Anthony. He always heard me. His head would pop up under the watering-can handle, and he'd squint into the sunshine. His triangular face reminded me of Sub-Mariner, a comic-book hero then.

My family didn't use Mad Anthony's watering can. We bought another one to water the garden with. But one time, somebody got mixed up and put water in Mad Anthony's house while he was out *boingg*-ing around somewhere. He came dashing across the lawn and leaped into the can. There was a terrible splash. And a long pause.

Then Sub-Mariner's dripping head appeared in the opening. His eyes were more squinty than usual. But he didn't say anything; he just looked casually around, pretending he wasn't up to his neck in water. He stayed in there for a long while just to make his point. Like I said, he was crazy.

I wish he were still around. Now, a lot of years later, I still think of Mad Anthony when I see tall grass. Or a watering can. But I never see a cat face peeking out. If I did, I guess I'd spring straight up in the air.

from Walter Chandoha's *Literary Cat*

Tales for Cats
by Russell Baker

My cat refuses to jog or diet and has no interest at all in tracking down Nazis. I mention this only to explain why I have become disgusted with best-selling cat books.

I bought three—"Jogging For Cats," "Dr. Pussikins's 18-day Cat Diet" and "How to Trap a Nazi With a Cat"—and Primrose (which is the name of my cat) turned his nose up at all of them.

Primrose was perfectly willing to go jogging, so long as I did the jogging and he was carried in my arms, but the minute he was set down on his own four paws he slunk into a thorny bush and sat there motionless, and no amount of shouting about his cholesterol-clogged arteries could make him come out.

I should note that Primrose is 15 years old and weighs slightly more than an overpacked suitcase. Dr. Pussikins's 18-day diet promised to shrink him down until he could once again get into a size-8 cat skin. We got his weight down all right, but after we did there was no way to get him out of his old size-38 pelt. As a result, a tiny little Primrose was left in such folds of sagging hide and hair that he looked more like a rug than a cat.

Fortunately, he wandered away from the house, was mistaken for a castoff rug and sold at a flea market. The buyer's wife said it didn't go with her other furniture and threw him out in the trash and garbage where Primrose was able to eat his way back to normal before wandering home again.

I was delighted to see him, since I had just bought "How to Trap a Nazi With a Cat" and was eager to train him for useful work. I had him out in the yard one day trying to train him to pounce when he spotted a swastika, and grandmother came out.

"What kind of foolishness is this?" she asked. I showed her the book. The chapter about how a cat, once properly trained, could track down and bring in the biggest Nazis in the book-publishing world.

"Imagine what a coup it would be if Primrose brought in Martin Bormann," I said.

"Martin Bormann!" she cried. "I've read about that fellow in several hundred best-selling novels, and he'd just as soon slit your gizzard as have a second beer with his sauerkraut. If Primrose is going to bring Bormann back here, I'm clearing out."

She had a point. I checked the book for suggestions on what to do with a Nazi once a cat had tracked one down and brought him in, but the author had ignored this problem.

In his youth Primrose had often tracked down birds and brought them in by mouth, proudly depositing them, half dead, on the parlor rug, then striding away and leaving them for me to deal with. That had been bad enough. Imagine him bringing me a Nazi, badly lacerated with cat bites and doubtless in an evil temper because of them, and dropping him on the parlor rug.

Primrose was happy about giving up training, and I was not terribly depressed either, since Nazis had gone into temporary literary eclipse by this time and the new best-selling subject was investment.

I bought a copy of the fantastically selling "How a Cat Can Survive the Coming Financial Catastrophe."

"According to this," grandmother said, "Primrose ought to be converted into gold or collectibles."

"It's the only sane defense against the coming financial catastrophe," I agreed.

"But if you do that," said grandmother, "we're going to have the house overrun with burglars as soon as news of the conversion gets around. If Primrose is converted to gold, I'm getting out of here."

This proved unnecessary. Primrose had been seated in the best parlor armchair during the discussion, and before it ended he climbed down, stalked out of the house and disappeared for several weeks. Grandmother, who believes Primrose has more sense than I have, said this proved that he was against being converted into gold.

During his absence I purchased the very latest best seller by the eminent psychologist Hugo Furrlein, "Conquer Your Enemies With Cat Power." I was mesmerized in the chapter explaining how to maneuver opponents for power into a chair covered with cat hairs so that when they stand up everyone will laugh at them trying to pick the hairs off their blue serge suits, when in walked Primrose with a best-selling author clamped in his jaws.

Primrose dropped the author on the parlor rug. He was exultant. "Primrose and I," he announced, "start work at once on a best-selling as-told-to opus to be entitled 'I was Hitler's barn cat.' Of course, we'll have to change Primrose's name to Fritzkin. Artistic license, you know."

"I always knew Primrose had more sense than you do," said grandmother, as Primrose carried the author off and began turning himself into gold.

from *The New York Times Magazine*
August 9, 1981

Pyramid Power

A lot of people are into pyramids; you know, putting razor blades and knives into them so they will stay sharp forever. Or they may have a triangle of mandarin oranges piled under a pyramid, still fresh from way before the war. . . .

I have recently read that some pyramid-power people have discovered their cats enjoy sleeping in pyramids [and are] more alert, able to play the trombone after only two or three lessons. . . .

I decided to try this out for myself. I built a lovely pyramid out of mahogany, carefully checked all the size specifications, and put it in the middle of my living room, sprinkled a trail of catnip to the entrance . . . and set up a lot of sequential cameras with little trip wires so I could document the entire experiment for *Scientific American*. . . .

I now have the sharpest cat on the block, proof positive that pyramids really do work. I've managed to get twelve shaves off one cat without having to put him back into the pyramid to recharge.

Not only that, but he can now open his own tins of cat food simply by sitting on them and rotating 360°.

There's a lot to this stuff. Don't dismiss it out of hand.

> Jurgen R. Gothe
> from *Cat Catalog*

I have an Egyptian cat. He leaves a pyramid in every room.

> Rodney Dangerfield

No More Mr. Nice Guy
by Russell Baker

Sometimes I wish I were Menachim Begin. Finding cat hairs in the salad bowl puts me in that mood. Every time

I find cat hairs in the salad bowl, though, I succumb to my natural instinct and whine about it.

"I don't see why the cats always have to crawl into the salad bowl and shed a lot of hairs," I whine. "I don't crawl into the cat bowl and leave a lot of whiskers, do I?"

And everyone sneers at me. "If you don't like a few cat hairs on your salad, don't eat it," they say.

People speak to you like that when you've got a reputation for being a nice guy. If I were Menachim Begin, it would be different.

"What's this? Cat hairs in the salad bowl again!" I'd cry. "All right, no more Mr. Nice Guy!" And I would seize the cats, lather them, reach for my razor and start to give them a close shave.

Oh, sure, everybody would make a terrible outcry. "Oh, please don't shave the cats, Daddy! Everybody will laugh at them when they go outside."

If I were Menachim Begin, I'd shave the cats anyhow. I'd point out that a shaved cat sheds no hair. That a shaved cat is a tough place for fleas to hide in. And why should anybody laugh at a shaved cat? They shave sheep every year, don't they, and nobody laughs at sheep.

Unfortunately, I am not Menachim Begin, or even Margaret Thatcher. Sometimes I'd like to be Margaret Thatcher. I'd like to be Margaret Thatcher when I find my kitchen invaded by two cats some moocher has sent over to my territory for a long residence.

If I were Margaret Thatcher, I would telephone the moocher and say, "You've got two hours to get those cats out of my property. If you don't move fast, I shall kick them in the kidneys."

I never say that, though. I say, "As a nice guy, I'm asking you please not to ask me to board your cats for two months," and the moocher always says, "There's nobody else to do it, so if you refuse they will starve to death in my absence."

Sometimes I wish I were the Ayatollah Khomeini. I'd especially like to be the Ayatollah Khomeini whenever I stroll into the dining room and find the cats licking the asparagus.

Unfortunately, I have neither the turban, the beard, nor the eyes to be the Ayatollah Khomeini, so when I cry out at the fleeing cats, "Those satanic beasts must be pursued to the ends of the city, slain and consigned to eternity in hell," everyone glares at me and someone always says, "It's not nice for daddies to cuss."

Oh, it's hard being Mr. Nice Guy, but even harder being Mr. Nice Daddy, and sometimes I wish I weren't. Sometimes I wish I were Leonid Brezhnev.

I especially wish I were Leonid Brezhnev when I catch the cats rubbing their fleas off into my pillow. Then I could boot them out of the house with two well-placed kicks and a cry of "Out, you running cats of capitalism, and take your fleas with you!"

Then when the cats have mewled to my associates about tyranny, brutality and aching hindquarters, if I were Leonid Brezhnev I would jeer at all pleas for kindness to cats and seize the animals by their scruffs, lock them in the coal bin and make them stand in line for hours for a scrap of food.

Because I am not Leonid Brezhnev, though, I am wounded when somebody says, "Kicking a cat is a terrible thing for a daddy to do," and I try to apologize to the cats by caressing them. The cats, who know a nice guy when they outwit one, withdraw. Their feelings are hurt. They will be lying in wait to bite a finger when I am dozing.

Sometimes I wonder if I am Ronald Reagan. I never

have a moment when I wish I were Ronald Reagan, but I wonder.

What brings it to mind is, the other night I delivered a major cat-policy speech at dinner. "This house has put up long enough with cat hairs in the salad bowl, cat tongues on the asparagus and fleas in the pillow cases," I said. "From now on, if we don't start getting respect from the cats around here, I'm going to blow up the entire house."

"Don't worry, kitty," murmured someone in the audience to a shuddering cat, "that's just nice old Daddy being grumpy again."

I had to admit to myself the child was right. I'd be a fool to blow up the house even though I do like to talk about it. Is it possible that I'm really Ronald Reagan? A pussycat who talks like a lion?

Sometimes I wish I were Menachim Begin.

from *The New York Times Magazine*
August 15, 1982

An Academic Cat
by Robertson Davies

In our ten years of existence we have had several cats here [at Massey College, Toronto, Canada], but not one of them has remained with us. They all run away, and there is strong evidence that they all go to Trinity. I thought at one time that they must be Anglican cats, and they objected to our ecumenical chapel. I went to the length of getting a Persian cat, raised in the Zoroastrian faith, but it only lasted two days. There is a fine Persian rug in Trinity Chapel. Our most recent cat had been christened Episcopuss, in the hope that this thoroughly Anglican title would content it; furthermore, the Lionel Massey Fund provided money to treat the cat to a surgical operation which is generally thought to lift a cat's mind above purely sectarian considerations. But it, too, left us for Trinity. Rationalists in the College suggested that Trinity has more, and richer garbage than we have, but I still believe our cats acted on religious impulse.

from *One Half of Robertson Davies*

The Cat in Music
by Claire Necker

The atom bomb fell just the other day.
The H-bomb fell in the very same way.
Russia went, England went, and then the U.S.A.
The human race was finished without a chance to pray.

If you know the song "The Cat Came Back," you won't be wondering why the above is the introduction to this summary of the cat's role in music. It's one of the last verses to be added to this famous song that was first published in 1893. Over the years, the tune has continued to gather extra stanzas, giving it far more lives than the cat itself. But always there's the same rousing refrain:

But the cat came back, couldn't stay no longer,
Yes, the cat came back the very next day.
The cat came back, thought he was a goner,
But the cat came back for it wouldn't stay away.

Cat songs are known to have been published since the seventeenth century, but none ever reached the popularity of "The Cat Came Back," probably because of its adaptability to almost any situation—even nuclear warfare. . . .

Many famous poems, like Wordsworth's *The Kitten* and Thomas Gray's *The Cat and the Goldfish*, have been set to music, as have cat nursery rhymes. Children's songs about cats have always been popular, and a listing of them would cover many pages. Then there are the special songs of famous cartoon cats like Felix and Sylvester.

Instrumental music with a cat theme is as plentiful as are songs about cats. Probably the best-known pieces are Zez Confrey's jazz classic *Kitten on the Keys* (1921), and Domenico Scarlatti's (1685–1757) *The Cat's Fugue*, both of which imitate a cat running over the keys of a piano. Other instrumental cat pieces include polkas, fox trots, marches, scherzos and schottisches. To appeal to the young piano player there are many simple but effective compositions, some with words.

. . . a good portion of instrumental cat music mimics cat vocalization. Composers have been giving us the equivalent of cat meows, spits, caterwauls—the works—since the seventeenth century, and they are so realistic in many cases that cats themselves are frequently fooled by them. A few ballets combine cat music with cat dancing. Tchaikovsky's *The Sleeping Beauty* is the most famous example: two dancers, portraying Puss in Boots and the White Cat, imitate feline movement while the orchestra meows and spits. Ballet itself honors the litheness of cats by naming [a step] after them: the *pas de chat*....

Cats have contributed more to music than lyrics and imitations of their vocalization and locomotion. They were furnishing music themselves from the sixteenth to the eighteenth centuries, when so-called cat organs were a popular form of entertainment. These consisted of narrow boxes in which cats were confined so they could not move. Their tails, which protruded from the boxes, were tied to cords attached to the organs' keys so that whenever a key was pressed, a tail was pulled causing the tail's owner to yowl. These yowls were music which so amused the audiences.

Not quite so barbaric were the showmen in the seventeenth and eighteenth centuries who trained their cats to be vocalists. At a given signal, which in one case at least was given by a monkey conductor, the cats meowed in concert. It makes you wonder how long it took the trainer to produce such a phenomenon.

The jazz world chose to incorporate the cat figuratively into its music. Early jazz enthusiasts began to call themselves *cats*. Negro *cats* became *black cats*, and other types of cats appeared when needed, such as the *hep cat* and *scat cat*.

from *Cat Catalog*

An Italian Music Lover

Fabio Tombari, particularly in his *Book of Animals*, talks at length about the many white cats he has brought up. One of his cats, Marette, was brought from China on board a battleship, and disembarked one summer evening at Pesaro in the arms of an Italian sailor. Fabio Tombari and his wife Zanze enthusiastically adopted this little grey velvet ball scarcely two months old. She rapidly became the uncontested queen of his closely-knit family. In a few months she revealed herself to be a great lady. "In truth, an aristocrat," writes Tombari. "She never meowed. If the wind ruffled her, she licked herself slowly from head to foot. She spent her time running around Zanze's room, sniffing the perfume flasks, poking her nose into the silver powder bowl to flour herself over, and immediately sneezing. She had a horror of mice and avoided them; she would only settle herself on cushions of silk. She must have counted amongst her ancestors some mandarin's cat, because she adored music: Boccherini, Chopin, Debussy, amongst others. One morning Zanze played us *Jardins sous la pluie*. Marette was in the middle of amusing herself with the pompoms on the curtains and had caught her claws in them. She tore away, ran into the sitting room and curled up in Zanze's lap, the better to hear Debussy. It was in just this way that she had one evening listened to Beethoven's *Pastoral*, breathing lightly, purring mutely in order not to disturb."

as given in Fernand Méry's
The Life, History and Magic of the Cat

Tut the Critic
by Priscilla Beach

When I wanted to find Tut, all I had to do was to start "Clair de Lune." Almost immediately Tut would mysteriously appear from nowhere and walk quietly over to the side of the piano, where he would stretch out in his leonine pose, with his front paws straight out. How he would listen!—not with sleepy satisfaction but with an air of rapt attention. The whole body was relaxed, except that his head swayed as rhythmically as a conductor's baton. If I wanted to dismiss my audience, I had only to start Bach's "Chromatic Fantasy and Fugue in D Minor." Tut would go like a shot out of a gun.

from *King Tut and His Friends*

The Sound of Music

Cats can be highly stimulated to sexual activity by sounding the note *mi* of the fourth octave. By use of the same sound, kittens, before puberty, can easily be made to defecate, but after puberty the sound loses its powers of bowel stimulation and instead becomes a powerful genital stimulant.

> Leon F. Whitney
> *Training You to Train Your Cat*

Classical Cats
by Gerald Fitzgerald

In the fall of 1982, Broadway yielded to the lure of the cat. A musical named *Cats* opened at the Winter Garden Theater, a long-running, wildly successful hit from London by the composer of *Evita*, Andrew Lloyd Webber.

With Classical Cats, London Records lets the felinophile hear other musical tributes to the cat. This delightful collection consists of fugues, waltzes, symphonic extracts, operatic excerpts, and songs. The music, written by several of the world's most illustrious composers, comes from many centuries, ranging from Scarlatti's to Copland's.

It has been said that some people dislike cats. If this is so, these misguided souls simply do not understand the creature. The cat, after all, is a complicated animal, and full appreciation takes time. But aided by this record, any doubter might quickly change his tune, and his fear or superstition turn to perfect love.

A collection of authentic folk material gathered and arranged by Aaron Copland (1900——) bears the title *Old*

American Songs. This is the source of "I bought me a cat," a simple, zesty piece brimming with good humor.

"The Catts, as Other Creatures Doe" was composed by William Lawes (1602–1645), a court composer in England. Its verse is satiric, describing amorous town blades. The reference to "Jeffry Lyons" alludes to a quarrelsome court dwarf.

In his fantastic one-act opera *L'Enfant et les sortileges* (1925), Maurice Ravel wrote a beguilingly lilting love duet for a White Cat and a Black Cat. His poet, Colette, provided him this unique opportunity.

"The Cat and the Mouse," a piano solo, has been Copland's musical answer to a Tom and Jerry cartoon. There is the expected wild chase, but the composer permits no M.G.M. finale: Tom eats Jerry.

"The Cat" is the fifth piece in a song cycle by Alexander Grechaninov (1886–1956). Written in 1920 to words by the poet Gorodetsky, the piece is a charmingly thoughtful character sketch of a scholarly cat.

All the world loves Sergei Prokofiev's symphonic poem *Peter and the Wolf* (1936). In this musical fable with narrator, the instruments of the orchestra portray the story's various characters: Peter (the strings), his grandfather (the bassoon), the duck (an oboe), the wolf (the horns). At one point, the stealthy cat (the clarinet), stalking through the grass, seeks to catch the bird (a flute), but the predator is thwarted by Peter's shouts of warning.

Camille Saint-Saens pays homage to many creatures in his *Carnival of the Animals*, a work not published during the composer's lifetime (1835–1921). The *Introduction and Royal March of the Lion* is a set of fanfares for two pianos and strings.

Benjamin Britten's (1913–1973) Festival Cantata *Rejoice in the Lamb* has a text by the eighteenth-century poet Christopher Smart, a religious man with an unstable mind. The words, written in an asylum, depict the worship of God by all His creatures. In the fourth section, Smart takes his beloved cat as an example of nature praising God by being simply what the Creator intended it to be.

Domenico Scarlatti (1685–1757), originator of modern piano technique, published his most significant composition, thirty sonatas, under the title *Exercises*. Legend has it that the theme for the final sonata, *La Fugue du Chat*, was created not by Scarlatti but by his cat, walking over the keyboard. A musical cat, considering its choice of notes.

The scampering Waltz in F, Op. 34, No. 3, by Frederic Chopin (1810–1849) may or may not have been inspired by a frisky cat. Many stories about the composer's compositions, after all, were invented without his permission by sales-minded publishers. Whatever, we like all those stories about raindrops, butterflies, and cats.

During Act III of Peter Ilyich Tchaikovsky's *The Sleeping Beauty* (1890), various fairytale characters appear to dance in celebration of Princess Aurora's wedding. Among the guests is Puss-in-Boots, who does a pas-de-deux with his pretty sweetheart, the White Cat. Using woodwinds, the composer paints a perfect picture of this feline pair.

Chris Hazell's "Borage," scored for brass ensemble, is a jazzy salute to a hepcat—one of the composer's own four feline companions.

The Pirates of Penzance has been a musical smash since it was first produced in 1880. Recently this Gilbert and Sullivan classic has played to sold-out houses on Broadway in an updated version, [now] on the screen as a movie spectacular. In the G&S original one discovers the popular song "Hail, Hail, the Gang's All Here"—in

fact, a chorus sung to the words "With Catlike Tread."
No more spirited selection could close this tribute to a
most distinguished animal, the Classic Cat.

from the jacket of a record album issued in 1982
(The author is editor of *Opera News* and
Ballet News and owner of two Siamese.)

Having a Ball

While Alice was sitting curled up in a corner of the great
arm-chair, half talking to herself and half asleep, the kitten
had been having a grand game of romps with the ball of
worsted Alice had been trying to wind up, and had been
rolling it up and down till it had all come undone again;
and there it was, spread over the hearthrug, all knots and
tangles, with the kitten running after its own tail in the
middle.

"Oh, you wicked, wicked little thing!" cried Alice,
catching up the kitten, and giving it a little kiss to make
it understand that it was in disgrace. "Really, Dinah ought
to have taught you better manners! You *ought*, Dinah,
you know you ought!" she added, looking reproachfully
at the old cat, and speaking in as cross a voice as she
could manage—and then she scrambled back into the
arm-chair, taking the kitten and the worsted with her, and
began winding the ball again. But she didn't get on very
fast, as she was talking all the time, sometimes to the
kitten, and sometimes to herself. Kitty sat very demurely
on her knee, pretending to watch the progress of the winding, and now and then putting out one paw and gently
touching the ball, as if it would be glad to help if it might.

Lewis Carroll (1832–1898)
from *Through the Looking-Glass*

"What is the appeal about cats? I've always wanted to know."

"They don't care if you like them. They haven't the slightest notion of gratitude, and they never pretend. They take what you have to offer and away they go." . . .

"He says he likes cats because they don't like anyone. I suppose he is proving he is so tough he can exist without affection."

Mavis Gallant
My Heart is Broken

There is not room to swing a cat.

Tobias Smollett (1721–1771)
Humphrey Clinker

I don't want to swing a cat. I never do swing a cat.

Charles Dickens (1812–1870)
David Copperfield

He shut his eyes while Saha [the cat] kept vigil, watching all the invisible signs that hover over sleeping humans when the lights are out.

Colette (1873–1954)
The Cat

"You know," concluded my cat, stretching out before the embers, "the true happiness, paradise itself, my dear master, is to be shut up in a room with meat in it."

Emile Zola (1840–1902)
Nouveaux Contes à Ninon

William The Copy Cat
by James Thurber (1894–1961)

A feline named William got a job as a copy cat on a daily paper and was surprised to learn that every other cat on the paper was named Tom, Dick, or Harry. He soon found out that he was the only cat named William in town. The fact of his singularity went to his head, and he began confusing it with distinction. It got so that whenever he saw or heard the name William, he thought it referred to him. His fantasies grew wilder and wilder, and he came to believe that he was the Will of Last Will and Testament, and the Willy of Willy Nilly, and the cat who put cat in catnip. He finally became convinced that Cadillacs were Catillacs because of him.

William became so lost in his daydreams that he no longer heard the editor of the paper when he shouted, "Copy cat!" and became not only a ne'er-do-well, but a ne'er-do-anything. "You're fired," the editor told him one morning when he showed up for dreams.

"God will provide," said William jauntily.

"God has his eye on the sparrow," said the editor.

"So do I," said William.

from *Further Fables of Our Time*

"Alf Todd," said Ukridge, soaring to an impressive burst of imagery, "has about as much chance as a one-armed blind man in a dark room trying to shove a pound of melted butter into a wild cat's left ear with a red-hot needle."

P. G. Wodehouse (1881–1975)
Ukridge

It was one of those cold, clammy accusing sort of eyes— the kind that makes you reach up to see if your tie is straight—and he looked at me as if I were some sort of unnecessary product which Cuthbert the cat had brought in after a ramble among the local ash-cans.

P. G. Wodehouse
The Inimitable Jeeves

Source Notes

Page

vi. L. Duffus: *The Cat's Pajamas*, W. W. Norton, New York, 1967.

3. Eric Gurney: *How to Live With a Calculating Cat*, Prentice-Hall, Englewood Cliffs, N.J., 1962.

3. Fernand Mèry: *Her Majesty the Cat*, S. G. Phillips, New York, 1957.

3. Edward L. Burlingame, quoted by Larry Ashmead in *The Cat's Pajamas*, by Leonore Fleischer, Harper & Row, New York, 1982.

4. Paul Gallico: *Honorable Cat*, Crown Publishers, New York, 1972.

4. Agnes Repplier: *The Fireside Sphinx*, Houghton Mifflin, New York, 1939.

5. Leonore Fleischer: *The Cat's Pajamas*, Harper & Row, New York, 1982.

5. *The Guinness Book of World Records*, Bantam Books, New York, 1978.

6. A. E. Hotchner: *Papa Hemingway*, Random House, New York, 1960.

6. James Boswell: *The Life of Samuel Johnson*, 1791. (Modern Library Classic, Random House, New York, 1964)

7. Leonore Fleischer: *The Cat's Pajamas*, Harper & Row, New York, 1982.

7. Doris Lessing: *Particularly Cats*, Simon and Schuster, New York, 1967.

7. Winifred Carriere: *Cats 24 Hours a Day*, Funk & Wagnalls, New York, 1967.

7. Paul Gallico: *Honorable Cat*, Crown Publishers, New York, 1972.

10. Arthur Schopenhauer: *Essays*. Translated by T. Bailey Saunders. A. L. Burt Co., New York.

10. Walt Whitman from "Song of Myself"

12. *The Book of Lists #2*, by Irving Wallace et al., William Morrow, New York, 1979.

13. William H. A. Carr: *The Basic Book of the Cat*, Grammercy Book Co., New York, 1971.

14. Steve Martin: from an early nightclub routine.

15. Ogden Nash: "The Cat," from *Many Long Years Ago*, Little, Brown & Co., Boston, 1933.

16. Ambrose Bierce: *The Devil's Dictionary*, from *The Collected Writings of Ambrose Bierce*, The Citadel Press, New York, 1946.

17. John P. Eaton and Julie Kurnitz: *The Disgusting, Despicable Cat Cookbook*, New Century Publishers, Piscataway, N.J., 1982.

17. David Taylor: *The Cat: An Owner's Maintenance Manual*, Unwin Paperbacks, London, 1980.

18. Charles Dickens: *The Pickwick Papers*, 1837.

21. John D. Macdonald: *The House Guests*, Robert Hale Ltd., London, 1964.

21. The first of William Cole's poems appeared in his *A Cat Hater's Handbook*, Pinnacle Books, New York, 1982; the remaining three are published here for the first time.

24. The Dizick quote is from *Dogs Are Better Than Cats*, by Missy Dizick and Mary Bly, due from Doubleday in spring, 1984.

24. Karla Brown's remark first appeared in Herb Caen's column in the *San Francisco Chronicle*, circa 1980.

25. "My Wonderful Cat," written for *Cat Scan*, is not autobiographical.

30. Beverly Nichols: *Cats' X.Y.Z.*, E. P. Dutton, New York, 1961.

30. William H. A. Carr: *The Basic Book of the Cat*, Grammercy Book Co., New York, 1971.

31. James Mason and Pamela Killino: *The Cats in Our Lives*, Current Books, New York, 1949.

32. Michael W. Fox: *Understanding Your Cat*, Coward,

McCann & Geoghegan, New York, 1974.

32. Louis MacNeice: *The Collected Poems of Louis MacNeice*, Faber and Faber, Ltd., and Oxford University Press, 1966.

33. Helen Powers: *The Biggest Little Cat Book in the World*, Grosset & Dunlap, New York, 1977.

33. Vance Packard: *The Human Side of Animals*, Pocket Books, New York, 1961.

33. Paul Gallico: *Honorable Cat*, Crown Publishers, New York, 1972.

36. Robert Stearns: "Dogs Are Not Purrfect," from *Cat Catalog*, Workman Publishing, New York, 1976.

38. Lewis Carroll: *Alice's Adventures in Wonderland*, 1865.

38. David Taylor: *The Cat Owner's Maintenance Manual*, Unwin Paperbacks, London, 1980.

47. Carl Van Vechten: *The Tiger in the House*, Alfred A. Knopf, New York, 1920.

47. Fernand Méry: *The Life, History and Magic of the Cat*, Editions Robert Laffont, Paris, 1966.

48. Tennessee Williams: "The Malediction," from *One Arm and Other Stories*, New Directions, New York, 1948.

48. D. H. Lawrence: "Puss-Puss," from *The Complete Poems of D. H. Lawrence*, The Viking Press, New York, 1964.

48. Jorge Luis Borges: *Ficciones*, Grove Press, New York, 1962.

49. Elizabeth Hamilton: *Cats—A Celebration*, Charles Scribner's Sons, New York, 1979.

50. "Advice From a Vet of the Future" was written for *Cat Scan*.

54. If this were a book about cows instead of cats, the limerick could build toward a truly awesome last

line. Substituting a cow for the cat in the second line, the poem could then end:

"Or Tad'll skedaddle on cattle that'll."

60. Théophile Gautier: *La Ménagerie Intime*. 1850.

61. J. K. Huysmans: *La-Bas*, University Books, New York, 1958.

63. Bill Hayward: *Cat People*, Doubleday, New York, 1978.

63. Doris Lessing: *Particularly Cats*, Simon and Schuster, New York, 1967.

68. John D. MacDonald, *The House Guests*, Robert Hale Ltd., London, 1964.

74. Thomas Hardy: "Last Words To a Dumb Friend," from *Collected Poems of Thomas Hardy*, Macmillan, New York, 1925.

76. Neville Baybrooke: "A Writer's Cat," as given in *Cats—A Celebration*, by Elizabeth Hamilton, Charles Scribner's Sons, New York, 1979.

78. Don Marquis: *archie and mehitabel*, Doubleday, New York, 1927.

78. Dilys Laing: "Miao," from *The Collected Poems of Dilys Laing*, 1967.

80. Paul Gallico: *Honorable Cat*, Crown Publishers, New York, 1972.

84. August Derleth: "Cat on the Hearth," *Collected Poems*, Staunton and Lee.

85. Theodore Roethke: "The Kitty-Cat Bird," *Collected Poems*, Doubleday, New York, 1975.

87. Aileen Fisher: "Half Asleep," *My Cat Has Eyes of Sapphire Blue*, Thomas Y. Crowell, Philadelphia, 1973.

89. Richard Shaw: "Squatter's Rights," from *The Cat Book*, Frederick Warne & Co., New York, 1973.

90. W. H. Davies: "The Cat," as given in *The Literary*

Cat, by J. C. Suares and Seymour Chwast, Berkley Windhover Books, New York, 1977.

91. Hal Summers: "My Old Cat," as given in *The Book of Cats*, William Morrow, New York, 1977.

91. Roger McGough: "My cat and I," from *Watchwords*, Jonathan Cape, Ltd., London, 1979.

93. Alexander Gray: "On a Cat Aging," as given in *The Book of Cats*, William Morrow, New York, 1977.

93. The couplet at the bottom of the page was suggested by Alexander Pope's "To err is human, to forgive divine"; S. J. Perelman's "To err is human, to forgive supine"; and Gabriel Weiss's (in the August/September 1982 edition of the newsletter *PURRRRR!*) "To err is human, to purr divine."

98. Helen Powers: *The Biggest Little Cat Book in the World*, Grosset and Dunlap, New York, 1977.

99. Eric Gurney: *How to Live With a Calculating Cat*, Prentice-Hall, Englewood Cliffs, N.J., 1962.

100. Fernard Méry: *The Life, History and Magic of the Cat*, Editions Robert Laffont, Paris, 1966.

102. Leonore Fleischer: *The Cat's Pajamas*, Harper & Row, New York, 1982.

103. Richard C. Smith: *The Complete Cat Book*, Walker & Co., New York, 1963.

105. Agnes Repplier: *The Fireside Sphinx*, Houghton Mifflin, New York, 1939.

105. Ashley Montague and Edward Darling: *The Prevalence of Nonsense*, Harper & Row, New York, 1967.

105. Nelson Antrim Crawford: *Cats in Prose and Verse*, Coward, McCann, New York, 1947.

108. Bill Blackbeard and Malcolm White: *Great Comic Cats*, Troubador Press, San Francisco, 1981.

109. *The People's Almanac #2*, by David Wallechinsky

and Irving Wallace, William Morrow, New York, 1979.

110. Agnes Repplier: *The Fireside Sphinx*, Houghton Mifflin, New York, 1939.

110. William. H. A. Carr: *The Basic Book of the Cat*, Grammercy Book Co., New York, 1971.

110. Georgia Strickland Gates: *The Modern Cat: Her Mind and Manners*.

111. Ashley Montague and Edward Darling: *The Prevalence of Nonsense*, Harper & Row, New York, 1967.

113. Helen Powers: *The Biggest Little Cat Book in the World*, Grosset & Dunlap, New York, 1977.

115. Leon F. Whitney: *Training You to Train Your Cat*, Doubleday, New York, 1968.

116. David Taylor: *The Cat: An Owner's Maintenance Manual*, Unwin Paperbacks, London, 1980.

119. Leon F. Whitney: *Training You to Train Your Cat*, Doubleday, New York, 1968.

120. Muriel Beadle: *The Cat*, Simon & Schuster, New York, 1977.

120. Leon F. Whitney: *Training You to Train Your Cat*, Doubleday, New York, 1968.

121. David Taylor: *The Cat: An Owner's Maintenance Manual*, Unwin Paperbacks, London, 1980.

123. Sidney Denham: *Our Cats*, Kaye & Ward, Ltd., London.

123. Steve Martin, from an early nightclub routine.

124. David Taylor: *The Cat: An Owner's Maintenance Manual*, Unwin Paperbacks, London, 1980.

125. Haskell Frankel, from the foreword of Louis Camuti's *All My Patients Are Under the Bed*, G. K. Hall, Boston, 1980.

127. Paul Gallico: *Honorable Cat*, Crown Publishers, New York, 1972.

128. Bill Hayward: *Cat People*, Doubleday, New York, 1978.

128. Winifred Carriere: *Cats 24 Hours a Day*, Funk & Wagnalls, New York, 1967.

129. Missy Dizick: from *Dogs are Better Than Cats*, coming from Doubleday in 1984.

129. J. C. Suarez: *Great Cats*, Bantam Books, New York, 1981.

131. Jim Davis in the foreword to *Great Comic Cats*, by Bill Blackbeard and Malcolm Whyte, Troubador Press, San Francisco, 1981.

138. Evelyn Underhill: from *The Letters of Evelyn Underhill*, Longmans, Green & Co., London, 1943.

139. Anne Frank: *Anne Frank: The Diary of a Young Girl*, Doubleday, New York, 1952.

140. Gilbert Millstein: "Cats I Have Known and Loathed," *The New York Times Magazine*, March 13, 1977.

143. Brian McConnachie: "Seeing-Eye Cats," from *Cat Catalog*, Workman Publishing, New York, 1976.

145. Derek Williamson: "Mad Anthony," as given in *Literary Cat*, by Walter Chandoha, J. B. Lippincott, Philadelphia, 1977.

148. Russell Baker: "Tales for Cats," *The New York Times Magazine*, August 9, 1981.

151. Jurgen R. Gothe: "Pyramid Power," from *Cat Catalog*, Workman Publishing, New York, 1976.

151. Russell Baker: "No More Mr. Nice Guy," *The New York Times Magazine*, August 15, 1982.

154. Robertson Davies: "An Academic Cat," from *One Half of Robertson Davies*, Viking Penguin and Mac-

millan Co. of Canada, 1977.

155. Claire Necker: "The Cat in Music," from *Cat Catalog*, Workman Publishing, New York, 1976.

159. Priscilla Beach: *King Tut and His Friends*, Harper and Brothers, New York, 1948.

160. Leon F. Whitney: *Training You to Train Your Cat*, Doubleday, New York, 1968.

160. Gerald Fitzgerald: "Classical Cats," excerpted from the liner notes of the 1983 London recording of the same name.

163. Lewis Carroll: *Alice Through the Looking Glass*, 1872.

164. Mavis Gallant: *My Heart is Broken*. 1964.

165. James Thurber: "William the Copy Cat," from *Further Fables of Our Times*, Simon and Schuster, New York, 1956.

Index

About the Authors

Novelist Robert Byrne's two most recent books are collections of humorous quotations called THE 637 BEST THINGS ANYBODY EVER SAID and THE OTHER 637 BEST THINGS ANYBODY EVER SAID. He is not now nor has he ever been a cat owner.

CAT SCAN and its title were suggested by Tẻressa Skelton, whose hobby is literary research. For a living she does computer-assisted design drafting for a gigantic public utility. She not only owns a cat, she likes it.

Artist Missy Dizick specializes in cats and permits galleries on both coasts to hang her paintings of them. The two cats she lives with at the present time are, she admits, flawed.

Cyra McFadden has had cats all her life and also wrote the best-selling comic novel THE SERIAL. She contributed CAT SCAN's Foreword because she needs no Introduction.